THE KINGDOM PASTOR'S LIBRARY

THE CENTRALITY of the CHURCH

Practicing the Ways of God
with the People of God

TONY EVANS

MOODY PUBLISHERS

CHICAGO

Some content in this book is adapted from *Oneness Embraced* (Chicago: Moody Publishers, 2015), *Kingdom Disciples* (Chicago: Moody Publishers, 2017), *Kingdom Agenda* (Chicago: Moody Publishers, 2013), *Horizontal Jesus* (Eugene, OR: Harvest House Publishers, 2015), and *God's Glorious Church* (Chicago: Moody Publishers, 2004).

All Scripture quotations, unless otherwise indicated, are taken from the New American Standard Bible®, Copyright © 1960, 1962, 1963, 1968, 1971, 1972, 1973, 1975, 1977, 1995 by The Lockman Foundation. Used by permission. (www.Lockman.org)

Scripture quotations marked KJV are taken from the King James Version.

Scripture quotations marked NIV are taken from the Holy Bible, New International Version®, NIV®. Copyright © 1973, 1978, 1984, 2011 by Biblica, Inc.™ Used by permission of Zondervan. All rights reserved worldwide. www.zondervan.com. The "NIV" and "New International Version" are trademarks registered in the United States Patent and Trademark Office by Biblica, Inc.™

All emphasis in Scripture has been added.

Edited by Michelle Sincock
Interior Design: Erik M. Peterson
Cover Design: Thinkpen Design
Cover photo of Bible study copyright © 2019 by Rawpixel.com / Shutterstock (1081710347). All rights reserved.

All websites and phone numbers listed herein are accurate at the time of publication but may change in the future or cease to exist. The listing of website references and resources does not imply publisher endorsement of the site's entire contents. Groups and organizations are listed for informational purposes, and listing does not imply publisher endorsement of their activities.

Library of Congress Cataloging-in-Publication Data

Names: Evans, Tony, 1949- author.
Title: The centrality of the Church : practicing the ways of God with the people of God / Dr. Tony Evans.
Description: Chicago : Moody Publishers, 2020. | Series: The kingdom pastor's library | Includes bibliographical references. | Summary: "The Centrality of the Church is the latest book in Kingdom Pastor's Library, a new series of books that brings you a succinct, complete pastoral philosophy and training from Tony Evans. Look for its release in 2020 or pre-order now"-- Provided by publisher.
Identifiers: LCCN 2019036385 (print) | LCCN 2019036386 (ebook) | ISBN 9780802418326 (hardcover) | ISBN 9780802496911 (ebook)
Subjects: LCSH: Church.
Classification: LCC BV600.3 .E929 2020 (print) | LCC BV600.3 (ebook) | DDC 262--dc23
LC record available at https://lccn.loc.gov/2019036385
LC ebook record available at https://lccn.loc.gov/2019036386

Originally delivered by fleets of horse-drawn wagons, the affordable paperbacks from D. L. Moody's publishing house resourced the church and served everyday people. Now, after more than 125 years of publishing and ministry, Moody Publishers' mission remains the same—even if our delivery systems have changed a bit. For more information on other books (and resources) created from a biblical perspective, go to www.moodypublishers.com or write to:

Moody Publishers
820 N. LaSalle Boulevard
Chicago, IL 60610

1 3 5 7 9 10 8 6 4 2

Printed in the United States of America

CONTENTS

INTRODUCTION

❖

As a pastor or church leader, you already know the critical importance of the church and the need for its impact on culture. You understand the role the church is to play in transferring the values of the kingdom of God into the everyday reality we all face on earth. I don't need to convince you that the church should be leaving an imprint of Christ's nature and attributes on believers as well as on society at large.

But what I may need to do, and what I hope to accomplish in our time in these pages, is to show you just how the church can function in order to fully flesh out her purpose. Weak churches leave little impact. Your role is to create the environment where your church not only grows and develops strong members through the process of discipleship but also equips your members to make individual as well as collective impact.

When the church is strong, its members recognize their eternal purpose, and the church moves forward. But when the church is weak, its members tend to wander around in confusion on their spiritual pilgrimage. My purpose and prayer for this book is that it will contribute to our understanding of the centrality of the church and the key leadership role of the pastor and church leaders. When our members become dynamic followers of Jesus Christ and contributing members of His church, we can and will transfer God's kingdom agenda values to the world as a whole.

CHAPTER ONE

THE KINGDOM

◆

In most recognized countries in the world, there is an American embassy, which is like a little bit of America a long way from home. Embassies have special immunities and protections from local law enforcement; the host nation's law enforcement can only enter the embassy with the ambassador's permission. If you get into trouble in a hostile country, make your way to the American embassy. Because once you cross the gate and enter the realm of its dominion, you are under the protection of the embassy.

The church is supposed to be a little bit of heaven a long way from home. It is to be that place where the values of eternity operate in history. The church is a place where weary people can go to find truth, acceptance, equality, freedom, safety, joy, justice, and hope. It is to serve as a centralized role in culture. Pastor, your job is not only to preach God's Word but also to administrate the critical operations of the church in such a way that your church fulfills its purpose in society.

Unfortunately today, far too many pastors lead their churches with a myopic view on the church's purpose. After all, how is it possible for the number of churches in our nation to be ever increasing while the impact of the church only wanes? How can we have so much preaching, praising, programs, and ministry resources and yet so little demonstrated power? Why does the church merely react to society's agenda rather than offering a kingdom agenda for its members, as well as for society, to embrace?

The answers to these questions lie in the reality that the church today bears little resemblance to the kingdom from which we came. This is because we have failed to function from a kingdom perspective. The church has stopped being the biblical church that it was designed to be, and as a result, we have limited our impact on contemporary society, both inside and outside our walls.

Throughout Scripture, God's agenda is His kingdom. The Greek word used for kingdom is *basileia*, which essentially means "rule" or "authority." A kingdom always includes three crucial components: First, a ruler empowered with sufficient authority; second, a realm of subjects who fall underneath this authority; and third, the rules of governance. God's kingdom is *the authoritative execution of His comprehensive governance in all creation.*

Therefore, the universe we live in is a theocracy. *Theos* refers to God. *Ocracy* refers to rule. A kingdom perspective means that the rule of God (*theocracy*) trumps the rule of man (*homocracy*). Psalm 103:19 expresses it this way: "The LORD has established his throne in heaven, and his kingdom rules over all" (NIV). Therefore, the kingdom agenda is *the visible manifestation of the comprehensive rule of God over every area of life.*

To understand your role as a pastor of a church and the church's centrality in our culture, you have to first understand the kingdom from a biblical perspective.

God's kingdom is larger than the temporal, political, and social realms in which we live. It's not confined to the walls of the church in which we worship Him. The kingdom is both now (Mark 1:15) and not yet (Matt. 16:28). It is among us (Luke 17:21) but also in heaven (Matt. 7:21; 2 Tim. 4:18), since it originates from above, from another realm. Jesus revealed that truth shortly before His crucifixion, when He said in response to Pilate, "My kingdom is not of this world. If My kingdom were of this world, then My servants would be fighting so that I would not be handed over to the Jews; but as it is, My kingdom is not of this realm" (John 18:36). While God's kingdom is in this world, it does not originate from this world.

Since it originates from another realm, God established covenants within the world we live through which to implement it. A covenant is *a divinely created relational bond through which God executes and administers His kingdom agenda.* These covenants are governmental systems or institutions designated as family, church, and civil government (state). God rules them all and each one is to be accountable to Him and His standards as their sovereign. Whether or not mankind functions in alignment with His rule is another story. Regardless, God has given the guidelines by which all three are to operate because He is the originator of all three. Failure to operate under His authority within those guidelines results in negative consequences.

The three, while distinct in their responsibilities and jurisdiction, are to cooperate with each other with the common goal of producing personal responsibility and individuals who govern themselves under God. None of these governing spheres is to be viewed or is to operate as an all-powerful and controlling authority over the others.

OPERATING UNDER GOD

The foundation on which all three institutional covenants operate is that of an absolute standard of truth. This standard of truth is nonnegotiable, non-adjustable, and transcends cultural, racial, and situational lines. Truth is fundamentally

God-based knowledge since God is both the originator and the author of truth.

Not only does the kingdom agenda operate on this foundation of truth, but it also operates under the only all-inclusive principle presented to us for understanding the work of God and His kingdom. This principle is His glory. Romans 11:36 says, "For from Him and through Him and to Him are all things. To Him be the glory forever. Amen."

Glory simply means "to be heavy" or "to have weight." It denotes significance. Since all things come from God, are through God, and go to God, God's glory exists intrinsically in Himself. Whether we ascribe glory to God or not is irrelevant to the amount of glory God has; His glory is already fully present in Him. However, we experience and access that glory when we place ourselves under His comprehensive rule. This is because it is then that God radiates and magnifies His glory to, in, and through us.

A primary position for bringing glory to God is that of surrender to His sovereignty. To surrender to God's sovereignty is to acknowledge His jurisdiction, along with the validity of His supremacy, over every area of life. God is accountable to no one. He either causes all things to happen or He permits them to happen. Sovereignty means that God never says: "Oops, I missed that one." When we lead our churches by the principles of the kingdom agenda, we experience God's hand in every area of our church as well as within our church members' lives and thereby witness His promise to work all things together for good (Rom. 8:28). As people are conformed to the image of Christ in their attitudes and actions, character and conduct begin to reflect Christ all the more.

However, what we often do is limit our opportunity to experience God working all things together for good by defining God according to our purpose rather than His. Humanism and socialism—whether it be in the form of modern-day church-ism, materialism, me-ism, statism, liberation theology, or Marxism—offers an insufficient understanding of the purpose, work, and revelation of God. It attempts to box God into a "kingdom" confined within the perspective of man. Yet, when the human condition is used as the starting point for seeing the whole of God's revelation, rather than a surrender to His sovereignty over the whole of the human condition, faulty theology and sociology emerge. What we wind up with is a God fashioned in the image of man.

A kingdom perspective does not view man's condition first and then assign to God what we feel would best reflect Him. Rather, a kingdom perspective ascertains how God has determined to glorify Himself comprehensively in the affairs of men and then aligns itself with that despite our inability to always understand God's processes. God is good, all the time. All the time, God is good. However, God's definition of good isn't always ours. In fact, God often uses the very thing that we call "not good" as a tool to bring about an ultimate purpose, as well as the resultant manifestation of His greater glory.

For example, according to the covenant with Abraham in Genesis 15, slavery in Egypt was an intricate part of God's program for the nation. We read, "God said to Abram, 'Know for certain that your descendants will be strangers in a land that is not theirs, where they will be enslaved and oppressed four hundred years. But I will also judge the nation whom they will serve, and afterward they will come out with many possessions'" (Gen. 15:13–14).

The point here is that God, in accomplishing His kingdom agenda, allowed a negative reality that could have been avoided if He had chosen for it to be. Yet the reality of the Israelites' slavery in Egypt accomplished a higher purpose of establishing God's theocratic relationship with them based on an exodus that would serve as a constant reminder of who had brought them out (Ex. 12:42). This truth served as a foundational relational principle in the future movements of God with the Israelite community.

God's sovereignty in the midst of what we do not understand is echoed elsewhere throughout the Bible. Another example is found in the life of Joseph who had been sold into slavery by his brothers. Joseph later said to his brothers, "As for you, you meant evil against me, but God meant it for good in order to bring about this present result, to preserve many people alive" (Gen. 50:20).

The freedom that is actualized through a kingdom perspective, that of embracing God's sovereignty, generates a faith and ministry perspective more powerful than any human weapon or system of philosophy could ever produce. It accesses God's grace in such a way so as to grant a freedom that is not incumbent upon externals. This is the only true authentic freedom as it manifests God's ability to bring about good in any and every situation surrendered to Him.

While God is a God of liberation and justice—and while we should be about the same—a kingdom perspective recognizes that in His sovereignty, His timing is not always the same as our own. However, a kingdom theology also recognizes that while there remain oppression and injustice in the world's systems, they should never be tolerated within the church of God or among members within the body of Christ.

In fact, whenever Jesus proclaimed the "kingdom of God" during His earthly presence, He did so while simultaneously healing, helping, feeding, and freeing the hurting and the lost. Therefore, any pastor of any church who minimizes legitimate social needs has failed to model the church he leads after the One whom we have been given to follow, thereby reducing the glory his church gives to God as well as its impact in the world (Matt. 5:16).

While we may not always understand God's processes or His timing, a kingdom theology recognizes that God's purpose does not change, and that purpose is to glorify Himself. The ultimate goal of the kingdom is always Godward. Therefore, living the kingdom agenda means that the comprehensive rule of God is the final, authoritative, and governing principle in our personal lives, family lives, churches, and communities in order that God may manifest His glory while advancing His kingdom.

THE SOCIOPOLITICAL DISTINCTION OF THE KINGDOM

The problem we face in the church today is that churches have misunderstood and undervalued the kingdom, thereby marginalizing its authority and influence not only in the lives of its members but also in our land. Many in the church have so spiritualized the kingdom that its sociopolitical rules have become little more than an ethereal ideology to be displayed at a later date. This has led to a reduction of the vast socio-ethical implications in the church, creating an organism whose function offers little power toward the transformation of its members and their impact in the world. However, the sociopolitical nature of the kingdom of God is very real, biblically substantiated, and relevant to the embracing of the church's purpose.

We first witness the sociopolitical distinction of the kingdom in Satan's challenge to God's rule. This challenge, while spiritual, was also political in nature in that it involved an attempt to secure a throne only God had the right to possess (Ezek. 28:11–19; Isa. 14:13–17). It was Satan who said, "I will ascend to heaven; I will raise my throne above the stars of God, and I will sit on the mount of assembly" (Isa. 14:13). Satan's desire to "sit on the mount of assembly" was his attempt to hold the seat of divine government in the spiritual realm while getting Adam to surrender it in the physical realm. From the beginning, politics was an issue in the rule of God.

Other demonstrations of the sociopolitical nature of God's kingdom include the command God gave to Adam that he was to "subdue" the earth under him, revealing the combination of the spiritual and physical aspects of a theocratic kingdom (see Gen. 1:26–28).

Next, the specific institution and creation of national government directly relate God's kingdom program to the social and political aspects of man as well, especially since capital punishment is instituted in this period (see Gen. 9:1–7). That capital punishment was predicated on the fact that man is made in the image of God (v. 6) underscores the truth that God's kingdom rule in the area of human justice has a spiritual and theological basis.

Further, under the patriarchs, Abraham was a participant in a covenant that included both land and seed. God promised to bless others through Abraham by making him into a great nation. This would come through the multiplication of his seed. Yet Genesis 15:18–21 also describes the portion of the covenant specifically dealing with the land promised to Abraham. This covenant became the basis for Israel's spiritual as well as sociopolitical existence (see Gen. 12:1–3). Likewise, whether in the conflict of Moses with Pharaoh, or in the judges, a theocratic role in governing the nation involved social, political, and economic forces as the means of expressing God's rule on earth.

Looking toward the millennial kingdom, Messiah's righteous rule, we also see a reflection of the social structure of the kingdom demonstrating the inseparability of the sociopolitical aspects from the spiritual. Christ's future rule will bring about changes within the structures of society. It will mean that military warfare will cease (Ps. 46:8–9; Mic. 4:3; Isa. 9:6–7), slums will be removed (Ps. 72:16), political wrongs will be righted (Isa. 2:4; Ps. 72:4), and physical disease will disappear (Isa. 35:5–6; Isa. 33:24).

THE CHURCH AS AN ALTERNATIVE MODEL FOR THE WORLD

The church is the nursery of the kingdom, housing its values and exposing them to the broader society. The biblical purpose of the church, then, in light of the nature of the kingdom, is to reflect the spiritual, sociopolitical, and socio-ethical aspects of the kingdom. It is to be a model for the world operating in the world while providing an alternative to the world. When the church functions as a kingdom community—not as a reaction to the world's ungodly system, but rather as a divine structure operating in a liberating manner according to the way God has ordained it to be—the church sets itself apart as a haven, much like an embassy. This then shows those who are in the kingdom of darkness a preview of what the kingdom of God is all about.

In the movies, previews advertise coming attractions. Designed to entice, the preview focuses on the hot clips of the movie such as the chase scenes, love scenes, and fight scenes. The point of the preview is to whet our appetites for the upcoming attraction.

Someday a big show is coming to town, and it's called the kingdom of God. God the Father is the Producer. The Holy Spirit is the Director. Jesus is the Super Star, and it will be a worldwide production. But until then, God has left previews of coming attractions in the world. We are His hot clips. God has left His church here to provide clips of the major production that is to come. Thus, the church does not merely exist for the church but for God's bigger goal which is the expansion of His kingdom.

Unfortunately, most of our clips have been so weak in demonstrating the power and wonder of the feature film that few people show interest in picking up a free ticket. Instead of previewing an epic, we often merely reflect the sitcoms and soap operas around us. Until we, as God's people, intentionally embrace, apply, and reflect the kingdom, the church has little to offer the world.

While there is war in the world, there ought to be the existence of peace in the church (Eph. 4:3; Col. 3:14–15), and prayer for peace by the church (1 Tim. 2:1–2). While there is oppression in society, there ought to be liberation and justice in the church (James 2:1–9). While there is poverty in the world, there ought to be voluntary sharing with the goal of meeting existing needs in the church (Acts 2:44–45; 2 Cor. 12:12–21). While there is racism, classism, and sexism in the world, there ought to be authentic oneness in the church (Col. 3:10–11). Thus, the world is presented with the option of Christ by being what the church is supposed to be in the world: an alternative model for the world—a community functioning under the rule of God in His mediatory kingdom rule on earth.

Members of the biblical church model this alternative on the basis that we are citizens of the kingdom (Col. 1:13), having been designated as workers for the kingdom (Col. 4:11), promised victory because of the unshakeable nature of the kingdom (Heb. 12:28), as well as heirs of the kingdom (James 2:5). Further, the fruit of the church reveals itself to others as the "good seed" sown during the period of the mysteries of the kingdom (Matt. 13:38). The church is therefore uniquely positioned and authorized to carry out the mandates of the kingdom under the authority of Christ (Eph. 1:22–23) when we seek the kingdom above all else (Matt. 6:33), empowered by the spiritual priorities of the kingdom (Rom. 14:17).

Since the church is to serve as a model partaking of this universal and eternal kingdom, and since this eternal kingdom is sociopolitical, flowing out of a biblically based spiritual foundation in nature, the church—as a spiritual body, led by kingdom-minded pastors—should also partake of the sociopolitical realm. The question is, then, what is the picture of the biblical church and its role with regard to justice? The next chapter will look at the centralized nature of the biblical church, laying the foundation for our discussion on the role of the church in personal lives and culture throughout the rest of this book.

CHAPTER TWO

THE MODEL

◆

Let me begin by saying what the biblical church is not. First, the church in the New Testament—which serves as our picture for the church age—is not a social club. It is not a place to come and be entertained. Neither is it an outpost for an official political party. While functionally it has sociopolitical structures and intents, it is never commanded to impose itself governmentally on the world.

The church, rather, functions as a model revealing the principles of the kingdom. The church is a community of individuals spiritually linked together with the purpose of influencing culture and reflecting the values of the kingdom of God through its members into the broader society.

The church is to function as a familial community with an emphasis on unity. By the biblical church, I am referring to the church that Jesus Christ established that is to be reflected or modeled through the local gathering of believers, a local assembly, as defined shortly before the end of His earthly ministry (see Matt. 16:18–19).

Several key verses in this chapter are very important for us to look at in order to understand who we are as a church and what we do. In Matthew 16, we begin by reading that Jesus had just asked His disciples an important question. He asked them to tell Him who people were saying that He was. Everyone offered flattering answers in reply. Some said that He was Elijah while others said Jeremiah or a prophet. While all were compliments, all were wrong. Then Jesus turned to His disciples and asked, "But who do you say that I am?" (Matt. 16:15).

It isn't evident in the English translation, but in the Greek text we discover that when Jesus asks, "Who do you say that I am," the "you" is plural. In Texas, we'd say, "Who do y'all say that I am?" The plural form of the word "you" reveals to us that Jesus is not just asking this question to Peter, who subsequently offered an answer. Rather, this is a question to the group as a whole.

When Peter answered, he answered representatively as a leader of the disciples. One way we know Peter is a leader is because whenever we see a list of the names of the disciples in the gospels, Peter is always listed first. He is a natural spokesperson both in personality and position. Peter doesn't have the paralysis of analysis. He speaks his mind and offers Jesus the collective answer, "You are the Christ, the Son of the living God" (Matt. 16:16).

Jesus responds by affirming him and changing his name, which had been Simon Barjona, to Peter—which means "a stone." He continues by saying, "And upon this rock I will build My church; and the gates of Hades will not overpower it" (Matt. 16:18).

Several important principles are given to us in this passage. First, the biblical church is *made up of many interlinking pieces*. Once the disciples individually recognized and agreed upon who Jesus was, they were ready to come together and be the church. This is critical because Christ is both the foundation and the cornerstone of the church (see 1 Cor. 3:11; Eph. 2:20–22). Once He saw that they understood who He was, Jesus esteemed their commitment to His identity by empowering them to carry out His work. He did this because their reply showed Him that they were a group of individuals who could jointly make an impact on society, which is exactly what they have done. Their impact has left a legacy that is still alive today.

What we sometimes do when looking at this passage, though, is make the mistake of interpreting Christ's statement as meaning that He is building His church on one man: Peter. However, the word Jesus used for Peter was the Greek word *petros*. It indicated a single stone that can be easily thrown. That is not the word Jesus used for "rock."

Jesus used the Greek word *petra* indicative of a mass—or cliff—of rocks that is comprised of something much larger than any individual rock. This mass of rocks interlinks individual rocks together to create a stronger whole. While there are a multitude of rocks in *petra*, they do not function as individual rocks, but are intimately joined together. The best exegete of the passage would have to be Peter himself. We see his interpretation in 1 Peter 2 where he says, "You also, as living stones, are being built up as a spiritual house" (v. 5).

It is not insignificant that Christ described the church in this way. Unity is an essential element used by God through which He manifests His power and reveals His glory. Therefore, if we, as leaders and pastors of churches, are going to be "the church" that Jesus is building, we have no other choice but to embrace our call to biblical-based unity across racial, class, preferential, and denominational lines.

Jesus did not place option B or option C on the table. He did not say that He will build a black church over here, and a white church over there, and a Hispanic church over here, and a National Baptist church over there, and a Southern Baptist church over here, and a denominational church over there, and a nondenominational church over here. Jesus did not give us that option. When we limit ourselves to those options, we have perverted His definition of His church. Rather, we are all individual stones coming together to form a larger, more complete whole upon which Christ, serving as the foundation and cornerstone, will build His church (see Eph. 2:20–22).

Second, not only are we all interlinking parts to one church, but the biblical church also has a ***culture-influencing capacity***. We learn this in Ephesians 2 when we look at the definition of the term *church*. *Ecclesia,* in common everyday Greek usage, originally referred to the land-holding citizens of the Greek city-state who had been summoned in order to establish the governance, guidelines, rules, and regulations for the broader citizenry. In other words, if you were a part of the *ecclesia* in the Greek societies, you were part of the governing council that legislated on behalf of the Greek population. *Ecclesia* wasn't a place where you came to sing a song or hear a sermon. *Ecclesia* was the place where you came to legislate on behalf of the populace. The word is even used this way once in the New Testament (see Acts 19:39–41), though by then, it had come to mean, more broadly, any group of people who were gathered for a specific purpose that benefits society.

Most of the time when we use the term "church" today, we simply mean a place where people can go to find encouragement, teaching, and fellowship. However, while those things are important, when we limit ourselves to them, we have reduced the word from its intended culture-influencing meaning. To be a part of the church of Jesus Christ, as Jesus defined it, is to be a part of an intentional body tasked to enact heaven's viewpoint and authority in the world's society.

In the midst of a place of war and conflict, God has deposited an *ecclesia*: a group of people who have been called out to bring the governance of God into the relevant application and practice of mankind. If you do not realize this or act on this truth as a pastor, then you are falling short of your kingdom role and responsibility.

This culture-influencing role of the church is clearly evident in this passage, since what is resisting it are the "gates of hell," which, in context, stand for the power of the evil one against which Christians strive. But the church purposefully brings God's way of doing things to earth, instead of Satan's way. This is reinforced by the fact that "keys" which are given provide access to heaven's authority to be executed by the church on earth (see Matt. 16:19). Jesus sits at the right hand of the Father to legislate from heaven, and we sit in the heavenlies with Him (see Eph. 2:5–6). God often waits on us as a church body to see whether we are exercising our legitimate authority or not. This explains why God determines what He's going to do from heaven in many cases by what He sees the church is doing in history and time on earth (see Eph. 3:10).

When the church settles for spiritual inspiration and information only, we wind up with temporal encouragement with little lasting transformation or cultural impact. The church is supposed to be where the values of eternity operate in history so that history sees what God looks like when heaven is operating on earth. The job of the church is not to adopt the culture, or to merely assess and analyze the culture, but to set heaven within the context of culture so that culture can see God at work in the midst of the conflicts of humanity as we develop kingdom disciples that penetrate the culture.

Third, the biblical church exists to **advance the kingdom**, not simply to defend it. Please notice the progressive nature of the language Jesus used. Jesus said that He is going to "build" His church. He did not say that He was going to stop hell. As mentioned in Matthew 16:18, "the gates of Hades will not overpower it." The term used for our translation of "Hades" is one we often interpret as hell—that which references the forces of the underworld, lower region, and realm of the dead.[1] Jesus declared that as He builds His church, the rulers of this underworld and lower region (the devil and his minions) will not overpower the church. Thus, it happens this way: as Christ builds His church, the inhabitants and rulers of hell see Him doing it. Hell does not like what Christ is doing, so hell tries to stop it. Jesus, and His church, is on the offensive. Hell is on the defensive.

However, for far too long, the church has operated on the defensive side of this battle. We've been reacting to the movements of hell rather than setting the pace of heaven. Jesus clearly says that the way you will know that your church is His church is that hell will be trying to stop it, and hell will be

1. "Hadés," Strong's Concordance, Bible Hub, https://biblehub.com/greek/86.htm.

failing. The reverse of that is true as well. The way you will know that your church is not operating as Jesus' church is that it will be only reacting to hell's advances, and it will be failing to stop them.

Jesus said His church will be hewed together around a common vision and purpose, making it not only capable of withstanding the strongest oppositional forces on the planet —the gates of hell will not prevail—but also able to make a progressive impact. However, if the church is not joined together as one, the reverse of that will occur as well, because that is the way Christ has designed the church to function. Without unity within and between our churches today (without compromising truth), the gates of hell—Satan and his minions—will overpower and engulf us.

If hell is on the doorstep, in the lobby, or in the pulpit and the pew of the church—which many would argue that it is—it can only be the result of the body of Christ failing to join together across racial, class, and gender lines as a unified whole in pursuit of a kingdom agenda. We know this is true because Jesus made it clear that He would build His church in such a way—and when done His way, the gates of hell would not overpower it.

That doesn't mean there is Christian uniformity, ignoring our different preferences in worship, music, preaching, fellowship, or even how long we want to meet together on a Sunday morning in what we call "church." The kingdom of heaven where we will one day go as the bride of Christ will be wholly diverse (see Rev. 7:9); therefore, we ought not to try to strip ourselves of our unique differences now. Rather, we need to welcome God's creative distinctions in such a way so as to make a stronger, more unified body in our land by joining church congregation and church congregation together, embracing an intentional strategy of edification through mutual service, thereby impacting not only our families and churches, but also our communities and nation, with the transforming power of Christ.

We must make the distinction between membership and fellowship. We can have fellowship with those who share the fundamentals of the faith, even if we can't share membership due to stylistic, policy, or preferential differences. The key point is the level of visible unity will determine the level of our cultural impact.

If we could ever see the kingdom as God sees it, and if we could ever see each other as God sees us, designed to come together with a unified goal underneath His overarching agenda, then the world would have to deal with the strength of the church of Jesus Christ. Now the world merely needs to deal with this segment over here and that segment over there as we divide ourselves over preferences.

Fourth, the biblical church operates with *full access to supreme authority and power*. The next verse in Matthew 16 says, "I will give you the keys of the kingdom of heaven; and whatever you bind on earth shall have been bound in heaven, and whatever you loose on earth shall have been loosed in heaven" (Matt. 16:19). Jesus says He will give the church the "keys of the kingdom of heaven." What do you do with keys? You gain access (see Isa. 22:22). Have you ever been in a hurry and you can't find your keys? That means that you're not going anywhere anytime soon. Or perhaps you are like me and you have a number of keys on your keychain, but you have forgotten what some of them unlock. Those keys are no longer of any benefit to you.

Jesus says the church He is building will have the keys to the kingdom of God, giving it the kingdom authority to bind and loose on earth based on its empowerment from heaven through proclaiming the gospel. The implications of this truth are staggering. If we could only grasp the potential of this reality, there is no end to the impact we, as pastors and leaders of the church, could have on our land and in the world.

Yet why are we not experiencing this power and authority in the church today? Because we are not operating in the way Jesus designed His church to function, according to His kingdom. We are operating according to "churchdom." Therefore, we are trying to use our own church keys to unlock kingdom doors and finding they don't open much of anything at all.

This reminds me of a time I flew from New York to Chicago. In New York, I had stayed at the Marriott Hotel. But when I got to Chicago, I went to another hotel. I checked into the hotel, and they gave me my keys. I made my way up to the twentieth floor and stuck my key card into the lock. A red light came on, so I tried my key again. A red light blinked again. At this point, tired from a long trip and not wanting to drag my bags all the way back down to the lobby to tell them that they had given me the wrong key, I'll admit that I got evangelically ticked off.

But down I went, making my way to the front desk. When I handed the lady at the front desk my key, she apologized and let me know that she would exchange it for me. Then she paused. Looking at my key card, she handed it back to me and said, "I'm sorry, sir, but this key is your problem. It doesn't go to this hotel." I had put my New York key card in my pocket, and once I arrived in Chicago, I mistakenly took that key out to try to open my hotel door. Understandably, it didn't work.

In other words, the keys Jesus is giving the church are the only keys that will work. These are not program keys, ministry keys, sermon keys, or song keys. These are the keys that belong to the kingdom of heaven. So if our churches are not kingdom-minded churches led by kingdom-minded pastors who are developing kingdom-minded disciples—if we have failed to comprehend, let alone adopt, a kingdom theology, ideology, and methodology—we will not be able to open heaven's doors. We will have prayer meetings, preaching, choir songs, and seminars, but no authority. We will have no authority on earth because the authority is directly tied to the kingdom. The keys belong to the kingdom. So if we are not kingdom-focused, the church will not possess and experience kingdom authority.

God's kingdom isn't here to take sides; it is here to take over (see Josh. 5). This principle can be further illustrated through a look at my favorite sport, football. Most people think that when a football game begins, there are only two teams on the field. That is a common misunderstanding. Each time a football game is played, there are three teams on the field: the two opposing teams battling it out for victory and the team of officials.

The team of officials, while in the game, answers to a higher authority—the NFL League office. They represent another "kingdom." They operate within the established purview of their own rulebook. You don't see officials on a football field asking the home team what it thinks about a certain play or penalty. You don't see them requisitioning a poll to determine whether or not the ball was trapped or caught. I've never gone to a game and seen an official ask the visiting coach if he thought his running back fumbled the ball or if his knee was actually down.

In football, the officials rule. They make the decisions. Bottom line: what the referees say goes. When they give their decision, they do so without hesitation because it doesn't matter to them who likes them. It doesn't matter to them who claps for them or boos them. The referees are not there to win a popularity competition. They are there to ensure order so that a victor can be ultimately declared.

Likewise, the church does not exist for the church. The moment the church exists for the church, it is no longer being the church. God created the church for the benefit of the kingdom. The church exists for the league office that sets the rules, governance, and guidelines that determine who the church is, what the church does, and how the church is to function on the game field of life.

God established the church to give us the keys to a whole other realm. He didn't place us here to be popular. Sometimes the crowd is going to boo us, but that's okay. We don't work for them. We serve a King from another kingdom who rules with supreme authority. Whatever God binds through the work of the church, the kingdom backs up just like the NFL League office backs up the officials when they make a decision on the field. Within the sovereign will and wisdom of God, a large degree of whatever we loose, the kingdom backs up. This is because the keys of the kingdom access the authority of the King.

Jesus only mentioned "church" three times in His earthly ministry, and all three times are recorded in the kingdom-focused book of Matthew (see 16:18, 18:17). The word "kingdom," however, is found fifty-four times in the book of Matthew alone. Yet, surprisingly, we often hear more about the church than the kingdom. We "plant churches" rather than promote the kingdom. Our seminaries teach our future leaders how to "do church" rather than how to be about the kingdom.

We ought to focus on both the kingdom *and* the church because they are interconnected. We can't have church without the kingdom. Yet the kingdom carries out its agenda through the church.

It is high time we become kingdom people as a church, representing something bigger than our own individualized groups and preferences. It is high time we made God's kingdom our rule and His glory our goal. God didn't establish the church to make us feel good. Rather, we are a people with a purpose made up of many members brought together in one body (1 Cor. 12:20), who suffer together (1 Cor. 12:26), and are fitly joined together (Eph. 4:16) in order to allow the full expression of the diverse spiritual gifts that have been given to each of us for the building up of the church for the impact on society, the opposing of Satan's forces, and the manifestation of the glory of God (Eph. 3:21).

Paul describes this when he compares us to a body:

> But to each one is given the manifestation of the Spirit for the common good. . . . For even as the body is one and yet has many members, and all the members of the body, though they are many, are one body, so also is Christ. For by one Spirit we were all baptized into one body, whether Jews or Greeks, whether slaves or free, and we were all made to drink of one Spirit. (1 Cor. 12:7, 12–13)

A danger in our culture today is that in our well-intentioned songs, events, and Sunday cross-cultural exchanges, we have idealized our call to unity as a church rather than embraced it. While campfire lyrics evoke sentiments of spiritual unity and connection, and that is important, it is never to be an end in itself. Unity is a means toward achieving a greater purpose of carrying out the will of God on earth "as it is in heaven." It is the environment created through the merging of diverse strengths through which the glory of God manifests itself within the power of God working in and through the people of God carrying out the purpose of God. Biblical unity is oneness of purpose, not sameness of persons.

Unless we view the model of oneness in this regard in how we lead our churches—as a kingdom strategy ordained by God against the schemes of the devil—we will continue to falter as pastors and church leaders simply because we fail to realize that the call to our role goes deeper than emotion. We need each other (see 1 Cor. 12:21–22). We are remiss not to embrace each other as God has ordained us to do, "whereas our more presentable members have no need of it. But God has so composed the body, giving more abundant honor to that member which lacked, so that there may be no division in the body, but that the members may have the same care for one another" (vv. 24–25).

If the church is ever going to make an impact on society, we must realize that we are a part of an established kingdom where God makes the rules. He has given us authority in the earth, but we are only able to exercise that authority according to His rules. Escaping those rules is as impossible as escaping the effects of gravity. Just like there are natural laws that govern nature, there are spiritual laws that govern the spiritual world. If you throw your phone out the window, it's going to crash to the ground. There's no way around it. Likewise, if we try to do church individually rather than be the church collectively, we're going to remain powerless and ineffective. This is because a preeminent rule for being the church is that we are unified. That is foundational: "There is neither Jew nor Greek, there is neither slave nor free man, there is neither male nor female; for you are all one in Christ Jesus" (Gal. 3:28).

Only when the church embraces diversity across racial (Jew nor Greek), class (slave nor free man), and gender (male nor female) lines and begins to connect with other churches in strategic ways will we be the haven God designed us to be in a world of lost people in search of a kingdom embassy.

CHAPTER THREE

THE MANDATE

◆

Submission to God's kingdom rule opens up the flow of heaven's involvement in our lives on earth through the centrality of the church. Yet far too many pastors and believers are satisfied with the part of Christianity that takes us to heaven, but not the part that brings a bit of heaven down to earth. But in order to bring to earth what "is in heaven," God's will must be done. Jesus' priestly prayer reflects this as well as reflecting His primary purpose while on earth, which was to be solely about His Father's business (see Luke 2:49). Since Christ is our example, we should be about the same.

One of the elements of God's rule and His "business" is His heart and mandate for oneness, also known as unity. As mentioned in the last chapter, unity can be defined in its simplest of terms as *oneness of purpose*. It is working together in harmony toward a shared vision and goal.

Unity is not uniformity, nor is it sameness. Just as the Godhead is made up of three distinct Persons—the Father, the Son, and the Holy Spirit—each unique in personhood and yet at the same time one in essence, unity reflects a oneness that does not negate individuality. Unity does not mean everyone needs to be like everyone else. God's creative variety is replete displaying itself through a humanity crafted in different shapes, colors, and sizes. Each of us, in one form or another, is unique. Unity occurs when we combine our unique differences together as we head toward a common goal. It is the sense that the thing that we are gathered for and moving toward is bigger than our own individual preferences.

SPIRITUAL UNITY

Through the establishment of the church along with His overarching rulership above it, God has created a reflection of His kingdom in heaven on earth. He has reconciled racially divided groups into one new man (Eph. 2:14–15), uniting them into a new body (Eph. 2:16), so that the church can function in unity (Eph. 4:13). The church is the place where racial, gender, and class distinctions are no longer to be divisive because of our unity in Christ (Gal. 3:28).

This does not negate differences that remain intact; oneness simply means that those differences are embraced. Joining our unique strengths together, we add strength to strength, making a more complete and balanced whole based on our mutual relationship with and commitment to Christ. So important is the mandate of oneness in the church that we are told to look out for people who seek to undermine it (see Rom. 16:17). In fact, God promised to judge those who divide His church (see 1 Cor. 3:17). This is because the church is to reflect the values of the kingdom of God to a world in desperate need of experiencing Him.

The church is the only authentic cross-racial, cross-cultural, and cross-generational basis for oneness in existence. It is the only institution on earth obligated to live under God's authority—and enabled to do so through His Spirit. In 1 Corinthians 12:12–13, Paul wrote:

> For even as the body is one and yet has many members, and all the members of the body, though they are many, are one body, so also is Christ. For by one Spirit we were all baptized into one body, whether Jews or Greeks, whether slaves or free, and we were all made to drink of one Spirit.

The baptism of the Spirit at the moment of salvation—the act whereby God places us into the body of Christ, the church—secures the oneness God wants us to have. This inimitable work of the Spirit positions us under the rule of God. We will look at baptism again later in this book, but for now, the Greek word for *baptism* used in the Bible means *identification*. When we got saved, we were baptized spiritually into the body of Christ. We are now identified with a new family, having been placed into a new spiritual environment while still on earth. No matter what our race, gender, or class, when we came to Jesus Christ, we entered into God's oneness because we came under His authority.

That is why Ephesians 4:3 says that we are to "preserve the unity of the Spirit." The Scripture uses the term preserve, indicating that we don't create unity. Authentic unity, then, cannot be manufactured. This is because God desires that His standards alone serve as the basis, criteria, and foundation for oneness. It is also why He thwarts attempts at unity that ignore or exclude Him (see Gen. 11:1–9). The Spirit created unity when we were saved. Our job is to find out what the Spirit has already done so that we can live, walk in, and embrace that reality.

Embracing that unity, or preserving it, doesn't mean simply sitting back and doing nothing. As we will see throughout the remaining chapters in this book, preserving unity requires an intentional action on our part. Sometimes that involves prayer. Other times it includes discipleship. Still other times it includes reaching out across racial or economic barriers to give unity an opportunity to flourish. Whatever the case, we are called to actively preserve unity among us, even if that means pursuing it through what we do. Preserving unity has much more to do with a mindset that unity already exists through the Spirit. It is our role to seek to allow it to thrive.

The reason we haven't solved the race problem in America after hundreds of years is that people apart from God are trying to create unity, while people under God who already have unity are not living out the unity we possess. The result of both of these conditions is disastrous for America. Our failure to find cultural unity as a nation is directly related to the church's failure to preserve our spiritual unity. The church has already been given unity because we've been made part of the same family. An interesting point to note about family is that you don't have to make a family be a family. A family already is a family. But sometimes you do have to encourage a family to act like family. In the family of God, this is done through the presence and power of the Holy Spirit.

A perfect example of spiritual unity came on the Day of Pentecost when God's people spoke with other tongues (see Acts 2:4). When the Holy Spirit showed up, people spoke in languages they didn't know so that people from a variety of backgrounds could unite under the cross of Jesus Christ. The people who heard the apostles speak on the Day of Pentecost were from all over the world, representing at least sixteen different geographical areas, racial categories, or ethnic and linguistic groups (see Acts 2:8–11). But in spite of the great diversity, they found true oneness in the presence of the Holy Spirit.

If we want heaven to visit history like what happened in the book of Acts, we have no other choice but to adopt and apply a biblical worldview, God's kingdom perspective, on oneness. We must view humanity through the lens of Scripture, seeing each other, as well as ourselves, as God sees us.

Admittedly, much has happened to mend the brokenness between the races in our churches over the last several decades, for which we should be grateful. I can distinctly remember how far we have come as it was only in 1969 that I was told by the leadership of a large Southern Baptist church in Atlanta that I wasn't welcome to worship there. In 1974, my wife, Lois, and I were informed in no uncertain terms that we were not welcome in a prominent Bible church in Dallas, pastored, by the way, by one of my seminary professors. In 1985, a number of major Christian radio station managers told me that there was little place for blacks in the general Christian broadcast media because our presence would offend their white listeners.

However, now I am routinely invited to Bible churches all over America to teach and preach. And today, my radio broadcast, *The Alternative with Dr. Tony Evans*, airs on more than fourteen hundred radio stations daily in our nation. We have come a long way in our nation toward oneness, but we still have a long way to go.

God's kingdom includes people from all races and cultures.

Spiritual oneness can only be accomplished when we expand our view of God's creation to see each other more intimately and clearly than our often limited exposure and understanding allows us to.

Satan spends most of his strategy and focus trying to divide us in the body of Christ. Why? Because he knows that God's power and glory are both accessed and magnified through unity. He is not spending his time trying to make the world wicked because he doesn't have to help the world to be wicked. The world is born in wickedness and division. Satan just has to let the world do its natural thing and then he seeks to use that worldview and the outcomes it produces to infiltrate the culture of the church. If Satan can keep Christians ineffective due to a lack of cooperation and mutual edification, he will prevent the church from providing a model of the kingdom of God as an alternative to its chaos.

If someone is an alcoholic, it is probably not a good idea for you to listen to that person on how to stop drinking. If the church is divided, Satan hinders our witness on the transforming and unifying power of God.

THE BENEFITS OF THIS MANDATE

Oneness brings with it many benefits. One is *power*. In fact, we see that even God recognizes how powerful oneness is when we read in Genesis 11 about the time when all of the people on the earth used the same language. They gathered together and decided to build a city whose tower would reach to heaven. But God then confused their language and scattered them over the whole earth because He knew that oneness is powerful.

Nothing expresses the principle of the power of oneness as much as this incident at Babel because if God recognizes its power and importance in history when embraced among unbelievers operating in rebellion against Him, then how much more important and powerful is it for us who are operating in harmony with Him?

Another benefit of oneness is that it *glorifies God* like nothing else because it reflects His image through His triune nature like nothing else. This truth comes through clearly in Jesus' prayer, commonly referred to as Jesus' high priestly prayer, shortly before He was arrested and crucified. He prayed,

I pray also for those who will believe in me through their message, that all of them may be one, Father, just as you are in me and I am in you. May they also be in us so that the world may believe that you have sent me. I have given them the glory that you gave me, that they may be one as we are one—I in them and you in me—so that they may be brought to complete unity. Then the world will know that you sent me and have loved them even as you have loved me. (John 17:20–23 NIV)

Jesus Christ placed a tremendous emphasis on His desire for us to be one as His followers just hours before He would lay down His life for us. This isn't something that He is asking us to do only during "Unity Month" or on "Special Oneness Sunday." This is a mandate from our Commander in Chief that we be one with Him and, as a result, one with each other.

A benefit of living out the mandate of oneness, as we have just seen in this passage, is letting the world know about the King under whom we serve. Oneness brings glory to God by moving us into the atmosphere where we can experience God's response in such a way that He manifests His glory most fully in history. All of the praying, preaching, worship, or Bible studies in the world can never bring about the fullest possible manifestation of God's presence like functioning in a spirit of oneness in the body of Christ. This is precisely why the subject found its place as the core of Jesus' high priestly prayer. It was the core because it uniquely reveals God's glory unlike anything else. It does this while at the same time revealing an authentic connection between one another in the body of Christ, which serves as a testimony of our connection with Christ. Jesus says, "By this all men will know that you are My disciples, if you have love for one another" (John 13:35).

An additional benefit of oneness is found in the Old Testament passage penned by David,

> Behold, how good and how pleasant it is for brothers to dwell together in unity! It is like the precious oil upon the head, coming down upon the beard, even Aaron's beard, coming down upon the edge of his robes. It is like the dew of Hermon coming down upon the mountains of Zion; for there the LORD commanded the blessing—life forever. (Psalm 133:1–3)

Unity is where the blessing of God rests, coming down from heaven to flow from the head to the body, and even reaching as far as the mountains of Zion. In other words, it covers everything. The reverse is also true: where there is disunity, there is limited blessing. We cannot operate in disunity and expect the full manifestation and continuation of God's blessing in our lives. We cannot operate in disunity and expect God to answer our prayers in the way that both we and He long for Him to do. Disunity—or an existence of separatism, from a spiritual perspective—is essentially at its core self-defeating and self-limiting because it reduces the movement of God's favor and blessings. Jesus made it clear that a house divided against itself cannot stand. Whether it is your house, the church house, or the White House—division leads to destruction (see Matt. 12:25).

Not only that, but a spirit of dishonor can lead to this same destruction (see 1 Cor. 12:22–26). Honor promotes unity while dishonor promotes division. Dishonor is not the same thing as disagreeing. A person can disagree with another person but do it in an honorable fashion. However, when dishonor is given to someone of a particular racial, social, or class background that has a history of the same, it negates attempts at unity.

Going deeper into Acts 2, we see the manifestation when the Holy Spirit moved like a "violent rushing wind" and "filled the whole house where they were" (Acts 2:2), in the midst of the oneness of the believers on the Day of Pentecost. At the end of the second chapter, the presence and product of oneness is emphasized as we read, "Everyone kept feeling a sense of awe; and many wonders and signs were taking place through the apostles. And all those who had believed were together and had all things in common" (Acts 2:43–44). Signs and wonders took place when they were "together" and "had all things in common." God manifested Himself when they were one.

What made this place and this period in time so electric was that the Spirit of God had taken over. The miracles that happened did not happen because the individuals had the best program, the best technology, or the biggest buildings in which to meet. They didn't have any of that. In fact, they barely had any income. No one among them had notoriety, a wall full of academic achievements, or charisma. They were simply common people bonded together by a common purpose across racial, class, and gender lines, thus receiving the Spirit's flow among them.

When they were one, God poured His blessing from heaven into history. God chose to do things that He would not otherwise have done if His people had not been one. Conversely, remaining in an environment of intellectual, spiritual, or social separatism limits the involvement of God's blessings in our personal life, family life, churches, and communities. We can overcome this separatism when we seek to preserve the unity of the Spirit through active means such as prayer, discipleship, and outreaches with the goal of strengthening the unity among us.

Achieving God's mandate of oneness is not as simple as reading a book about it. Just as a husband and wife must give up a lot to gain the oneness that marriage offers, so the races must be willing to pay the price of spiritual oneness. All sides must be willing to experience the potential rejection of friends and relatives, whether Christians or non-Christians, who are not willing to accept that spiritual family relationships transcend physical, cultural, and racial relationships. This is what Jesus meant when He said, "Whoever does the will of My Father who is in heaven, he is My brother and sister and mother" (Matt. 12:50).

Pastors and spiritual leaders must actively remind our congregations of Ephesians 2:14–22:

> For He Himself is our peace, who made both groups into one and broke down the barrier of the dividing wall, by abolishing in His flesh the enmity, which is the Law of commandments contained in ordinances, so that in Himself He might make the two into one new man, thus establishing peace, and might reconcile them both in one body to God through the cross, by it having put to death the enmity. And He came and preached peace to you who were far away, and peace to those who were near; for through Him we both have our access in one Spirit to the Father. So then you are no longer strangers and aliens, but you are fellow citizens with the saints, and are of God's household, having been built on the foundation of the apostles and prophets, Christ Jesus Himself being the corner stone, in whom the whole building, being fitted together, is growing into a holy temple in the Lord, in whom you also are being built together into a dwelling of God in the Spirit.

This passage makes the mandate of oneness first and foremost theological, not simply social. Jesus Christ died so that we might be unified as "one new man" in "one body" having access to God in "one Spirit." The absence of the oneness that Jesus died to bring hinders God's involvement and work in the church because the Holy Spirit occupies the church, and His work is directly tied to our unity.

Important as preaching is, it is not enough. Important as teaching and cultural-awareness seminars are, they are not enough. Important as books on unity are, they are not enough. The church must follow up with practical opportunities for bridging the cultural divide through mutual acts of service. The time has come to take an active role in inviting not only God's favor but also His blessing into our churches and lives through the intentional pursuit of oneness in the body of Christ. Nothing will bond people together more than hearts that reflect God's heart of oneness. This should naturally produce an outgrowth of working together in mutual acts of service while striving toward common goals.

It is high time for a transformation in the body of Christ. It is high time to rip off the tainted lenses of tradition in order to see each other, and ourselves, for who we truly are: valuable members of one another made in the exquisite image of our God. It is high time to intentionally pray toward a greater unity among us and then seek God and His guidance on how to specifically pursue it within our own spheres of influence. Only then can the church accurately reflect its spiritual content in this age in such a way that the world can clearly see an alternative to the brokenness of our current state. Having seen this alternative and responded to it, individuals, families, and communities will then be placed in the sphere where they too can experience a bit of heaven on earth until the fullness of heaven comes to earth at the second coming of Jesus Christ.

So many individuals today live segmented, compartmentalized lives because they lack implementation of God's kingdom worldview and subsequently lack the blessings of His Shekinah glory operating in our midst. Families disintegrate because they exist for their own satisfaction rather than for the kingdom. Churches are limited in the scope of their impact because they fail to comprehend that the goal of the church is not the church itself, but the kingdom. Communities have nowhere to turn to find real solutions for real people who have real problems because the church has become divided and ingrown, making it unable to significantly transform the cultural landscape. When our spiritual relationship to God and His rule is no longer the final and authoritative standard under which all else falls, then everything else is up for grabs.

But the reverse of that is true as well: As long as there is God, there is hope. He's the only one you or I can truly bank on. As long as God is still in the picture, and as long as His agenda is still on the table, it's not over. As long as God, and His rule, is still present in our churches, there is hope. But in a world where everyone is divided around their own cultural ideas, we end up losing the very thing that can carry us through each day: hope. When truth loses meaning, we cannot be sure about anything. This makes it difficult to find hope since truth, ultimately, is the centerpiece of hope.

I live in Dallas, Texas, and in Dallas, there is a loop that I take when I want to get somewhere on the other side of the city but don't necessarily want to head straight through downtown. This loop will take me close enough to the city so that I can see its towering buildings and skyline, but not close enough to actually experience it.

This is precisely what we, as pastors leading a church culture, have done with God regarding oneness in the body of Christ. We have put God on the "loop" of our lives. He is close enough to be at hand should we need His call for oneness in a national emergency but far enough away that He can't be the centrality of who we are each and every day in our local churches. Therefore, He will not bring hope or deliverance.

It doesn't take much more than a cursory glance around our society today to realize that our world is in desperate need of hope. Our communities need hope. Our world needs hope. It's the central focus of the church to be a vehicle to deliver that hope when it is rooted in the truth of God's Word, carrying out the mandate of oneness in Christ.

CHAPTER FOUR

THE MISSION

◆

If you have a smartphone, it is likely that you have a password restriction on your smartphone so that if you inadvertently left it somewhere, a stranger—or a friend—couldn't pick it up and take advantage of the personal information that is on your phone. Knowing a password allows access to something, and the password for the centrality of the church is *discipleship*.

In one of my favorite chapters in Scripture, Paul gives us the visual illustration of what it means to be a disciple. It starts with surrendering all of life to the Lordship of Jesus Christ. We read,

> Therefore, I urge you, brothers and sisters, in view of God's mercy, to offer your bodies as a living sacrifice, holy and pleasing to God—this is your true

and proper worship. Do not conform to the pattern of this world, but be transformed by the renewing of your mind. Then you will be able to test and approve what God's will is—his good, pleasing and perfect will. (Romans 12:1–2 NIV)

The problem with many Christians is that while they have made a decision to become a Christian by trusting in Jesus Christ for their salvation, they have not grown much in obedience as a disciple of Christ. The difference between a decision-maker and an obedient disciple is simply *surrender*.

BECOMING A KINGDOM DISCIPLE

Kingdom disciples are in such short supply today that the results are a bevy full of powerless Christians attending powerless churches led by powerless pastors resulting in a powerless presence in the world. Until this foundational principle called discipleship is recovered and utilized, we will continue to fail in our calling to adequately live as heaven's representatives on earth. The power, authority, abundance, victory, and impact promised in God's Word to His own will only be ours when we understand and align ourselves with His definition of discipleship. Until then, we can anticipate that disaster will continue to be the norm in spite of all the Christian activities we engage in.

Discipleship is the missing key to a life of authority under

God. But surrender to Christ's Lordship and obedience to His rule of love are the grooves and edges which make up that key, that when used rightly will unlock the power to bring heaven to bear on earth.

A kingdom disciple can be defined as *a believer in Christ who takes part in the spiritual developmental process of progressively learning to live all of life under the Lordship of Jesus Christ.* The goal of a kingdom disciple is to have a transformed life that transfers the values of the kingdom of God so that they replicate themselves in the lives of others. The result of such replication is God's exercising His rule from heaven to history through His kingdom disciples.

But there's more to discipleship than the personal dimension of our spiritual growth in grace. It also involves the local church and your role as a pastor or church leader. That's why, for the church, discipleship is *the developmental process of the local church by which Christians are brought from spiritual infancy to spiritual maturity, so that they can reproduce the process with others,* which the Bible calls being "conformed to the image of [God's] Son" (Rom. 8:29). This verse is crucial because it goes on to explain the goal of our becoming like Jesus Christ: "So that He would be the firstborn among many brethren."

In other words, the process of spiritual development has in view a discipleship that leads to believers becoming Christlike and that is designed to be repeated again and again in your church and through your members until Jesus has many brothers and sisters who look like Him. You and I can't do this if we are living as isolated Christians. Someone has said that Christianity was never meant to be "Jesus and me, under a tree." God placed us in a body of people called the church so that together we can accomplish the mission. The church is God's place to produce disciples who think and talk and act so much like Jesus that the world can look at us and say, "This must be what Jesus is like." Jesus Himself said, "It is enough for the disciple that he become like his teacher" (Matt. 10:25).

We have Jesus' authority and command to make disciples as Christians. This is exciting because it means that He is with us in the process to ensure that it works when we do it right. Here's an illustration that may help put this matter of discipleship in a familiar context.

The sermons I preach at our church in Dallas are recorded on a master file. These masters are then put on a duplicating machine to produce CDs and MP3s for our church members and to go out all over the world through our national ministry, The Urban Alternative.

There is only one master file for each message, but of course this master can produce any number of duplicates. It's interesting that the duplicating machine into which the blank CDs are placed to receive the master file's message is called the "slave unit." The task of the slave unit is not to create its own message, or to distort the message it is receiving, but to faithfully record and play back what is said on the master file.

That's a picture of the discipleship process. Jesus is the Master, and we are His slaves, the bearers of the message of the Master (see Eph. 6:6). Even though we are not the master, we can put others in touch with the Master by faithfully delivering His message. The goal is to reproduce the master as completely and faithfully as possible so that the correct message gets through to each listener each time one of the duplicates is played.

DISCIPLESHIP IN
THE GREAT COMMISSION

Jesus' first words to His disciples in Matthew 28:18 are indispensable to the church's ability to execute its mission. I love this declaration: "All authority has been given to Me in heaven and on earth." Evans's translation: "I am in charge now."

The word Jesus used for *authority* means "authority in legitimate hands." In other words, Jesus is not only in charge in the universe, but He is *rightfully* in charge. His authority was given to Him by God the Father by virtue of Christ's death and resurrection in victory over sin, death, and the devil. And Jesus is now in charge both "in heaven and on earth," in time and eternity. His authority is complete and eternal. Read the book of Revelation, and you'll see that no one is ever going to unseat Him.

With His disciples worshiping Him and His authority established, Jesus gave them—and us—a commission to carry out until the end of the age: "Go therefore and make disciples of all the nations" (Matt. 28:19). Making disciples is not part of the gospel in the sense that it is not an integral part of what a person needs to know to be justified. But we need to understand that our salvation is not the be-all and end-all of what God wants to do with us. It is not the end of the process, but the beginning. Our calling isn't complete until the church is making disciples who can go and make more disciples. Conversion is the free entrance into Jesus' school of discipleship and every believer is expected to attend class.

We stopped our reading at verse 19 because it is the core of the commission. The phrase "make disciples" is a command in the Greek, and in fact it is the only command in this text. The other three activities—going, baptizing, and teaching—are actually participles that explain and expand the command to make disciples.

I'm afraid that too many pastors have become so familiar with spiritual jargon that we have forgotten what an awesome concept making disciples really is. Jesus committed His entire enterprise for this age to the church—to people like you and me. What's more, He told us to take it to "all the nations." Discipleship is so big that when we are obedient to God and faithful in discipling people, the church will impact the world. While the church is often waiting on God to move, God—and the world—is waiting on the church.

The Greek word translated *disciple* in the New Testament was not a uniquely Christian term. It means "student" or learner, and the practice of making disciples was well known in the Greek world hundreds of years before Christ. This Greek discipleship system was very effective, because even after Rome conquered Greece, the Romans could not eradicate Greek influence. So, while Rome wielded military power, the Greeks wielded power over the culture because well-trained Greek disciples were functioning at every level of the society. This Greek influence was known as the hellinization of Rome. These people lived under Roman rule, but their thinking was Greek. And in the end, what people think is a lot more important and powerful than what an external power can force them to do.

This helps us understand why Jesus commissioned the church to make disciples. When it's done right, the disciple becomes a follower for life because the real battle for souls is waged in the mind. A well-trained disciple can live in a foreign, hostile culture without succumbing to that culture because his mind is fixed on God's kingdom.

God has called out of the world a body of people known as the church, men and women and young people who live under the lordship of Jesus Christ. He wants us, as disciples, to make other disciples who can then be sent out into this world to infiltrate its structures and bring the thinking of Christ to bear on every part of society until every nation has been discipled.

That's why the church must train Christians to be in the arts and entertainment, and in politics, law, economics, and education to introduce Jesus Christ to a world that does not know Him. A person's greatest influence is wherever Christ has placed them to represent Him.

Before we go any further, let's read the "minutes" of Jesus' meeting with the disciples:

> The eleven disciples proceeded to Galilee, to the mountain which Jesus had designated. When they saw Him, they worshiped Him; but some were doubtful. And Jesus came up and spoke to them, saying, "All authority has been given to Me in heaven and on earth. Go therefore and make disciples of all the nations, baptizing them in the name of the Father and the Son and the Holy Spirit, teaching them to observe all that I commanded you; and lo, I am with you always, even to the end of the age." (Matt. 28:16–20)

I'll bet you have never read any church committee minutes like those before. But despite the fact that this meeting includes all the saints in church history from Pentecost to today, I want to suggest that one of the problems in the church that is standing in our way of restoring the culture is this: We don't have enough committed followers of Jesus Christ. Kingdom disciples are in short supply.

Now if there is a discipleship problem in the church, we can be sure it has nothing to do with the church's Head and the Leader of this meeting, Jesus Christ. In fact, Jesus said that "all authority" had been given to Him in heaven and on earth.

So according to Jesus, a disciple's first concern should be that God's will is done on earth just as it is done in heaven. How is God's will done in heaven? Completely and perfectly, no questions, no objections, no debate. In fact, Satan was the only one to ever challenge God's will in heaven, and he was kicked out.

Jesus' plan is that there be a group of people who function as His legal representatives to reflect and implement God's will on earth. This would be the role and responsibility of kingdom disciples. The discipleship process is designed to extend Jesus' authority to and through His followers. That way, no matter where people live, if they want to know what is going on in heaven, all they have to do is check out the lives of believers individually and collectively. God's people are to be exercising heaven's authority in history. Kingdom discipleship and authority go hand in hand (see Luke 9:1–2; 1 Cor. 4:20) and involves the transfer of the rule of our King and His kingdom to the world over which He has been given authority.

Since Jesus has already achieved victory and Satan is a defeated enemy, what is our role as followers of His here on earth? Jesus answered that in Matthew 28, but He also gave a very succinct answer on one occasion when He and the disciples were nearing Jerusalem just before His crucifixion.

The disciples thought that Jesus was going to Jerusalem to take over and set up His kingdom right then. Jesus knew what they were thinking, so He told them the parable of the nobleman who went on a long journey and left certain sums of money with his servants. Then the nobleman said something very interesting. He told them, "Occupy till I come" (Luke 19:13 KJV). In other words, "Do business for me while I'm gone. I'll be back."

I like that word "occupy." As Jesus' disciples, we're like the occupying army that a conquering general leaves behind in the conquered country to maintain stability and progression after the battle has been won. Even though Satan is a defeated enemy, he has still got a lot of fight left in him, and he wants to take as many people down with him as he can. So our task as Jesus' occupying force is more involved than just sitting back and keeping an eye on things. The purpose of the church is to make disciples, not just increase Bible study attendance. It's not enough for the church just to be open a certain number of hours a week or offer a variety of programs. We are to make disciples.

Keep in mind, a kingdom disciple is a person who has decided that following Jesus Christ takes precedence over everything else in life. A disciple looks like the one he or she follows. A disciple intentionally chooses Christ and His will over their own, even at their own personal expense. Being a kingdom disciple demands submission and surrender to the Lordship of Jesus Christ in every area of life. This impacts the way we choose to spend our time, talents, and treasures for God and His glory rather than our own. But also remember that our inheritance in the kingdom will be determined by the degree of faithfulness with which we serve the King as His disciple here and now (see 2 Cor. 5:10).

Jesus never said that being a disciple would be easy. While becoming a Christian is without a cost, growing in your walk as a kingdom disciple demands a cost. In Mark 8:34–36, Jesus made one of the most profound statements in all of Scripture:

> If anyone wishes to come after Me, he must deny himself, and take up his cross and follow Me. For whoever wishes to save his life will lose it, but whoever loses his life for My sake and the gospel's will save it. For what does it profit a man to gain the whole world, and forfeit his soul?

How do you wish to save your life yet lose it? By going after the world. When you do that, you forfeit your life because life consists of more than the stuff you accumulate or positions you hold. Many people have a house but no longer have a home. Many people have money but don't have peace. Many people have plans but don't have any purpose. This principle of saving and losing your life is fixed. It's another way of saying you can't find God's purpose for your life when you're busy trying to find your own.

Years ago when the military draft was still in operation, young men were often called into the service at very inopportune times. For example, it didn't matter if you had just gotten married. It was good-bye bride, hello Uncle Sam. The same was true if the draftee just got a great job. But this new draftee did more than just leave family and friends behind. He now became the property of the U.S. government. His new master dictated every detail of his life: when to get up and go to bed, what to eat—even how to dress, stand, and walk.

After boot camp, the military took a further step in controlling this soldier's life. It selected a new location for him to live, usually far from home, and a new occupation. If there was a war going on, this soldier could be sent to the front lines where he might be killed.

If young men could be expected to sacrifice everything for their country, how much more should we as believers be willing to do whatever our Commander in Chief, Jesus Christ, asks of us? That's what is expected of us as His followers. Jesus is not looking for fans but for committed followers. Jesus wants full-time followers, not part-time saints. Giving yourself totally to God is giving Him full power over your life as His follower. When you do that, you experience the abundant life He has promised to give you.

Of course, not everyone who heard Jesus speak while He was on earth became His disciple. Whenever Jesus drew a large crowd, He eliminated most of them by talking about the requirements of following Him. If Jesus were interested in just building a large fan base, He would have kept quiet about the cost of discipleship.

But Jesus wasn't playing the numbers game. He was making disciples. Unfortunately, most of the people who heard Him weren't interested in absolute commitment to His authority. Getting by was good enough for them. Sadly, that's too often the case with Christians today. Too many of us serve Christ as long as He doesn't start messing with our comfort. We're willing to follow Him as long as He keeps money in our pockets and smiles on our faces. We don't want to be inconvenienced.

> "Yes, I love the Lord, but I'm not really interested in serving others."

> "I want to serve God, but my job keeps me too busy."

> "Wednesday prayer meeting is during my favorite television program. But I'll give God two good hours on Sunday."

Few church members would ever say things like this out loud, but that's the message they convey. As a result, there are too few disciples around to enable the church to impact the world. We have plenty of pastors, church buildings, members, and activities. But where are the true followers? Where are the men and women who understand that their purpose is to represent God's kingdom in every area of life?

This shortage of disciples explains why we have so many Christians and so little impact within our own churches, let alone in the country at large. What we need now are not more bodies in the pews. What we desperately need are more disciples, visible and verbal unapologetic followers of Jesus Christ. If we are going to see our country change, it will be because we make disciples in obedience to Christ's command and see them exercise the authority of heaven in history.

Until we become disciples ourselves and make disciples, we cannot hope to see change. The church in America will remain weak and ineffective, resulting in the continual deterioration of the culture. But there's still hope that the church can get its strength back if it moves to a focus on discipleship.

Notice in Matthew 28:19 that Jesus told the people who were gathered at that meeting in Galilee to make disciples "of all the nations." So the concern of discipleship is not just for individuals but also for systems that affect people's lives, including government. That was a big job even when the known world was just the Roman Empire. In order for them to do that, those early disciples would have to be big dreamers and mighty doers. They would need to possess and carry out kingdom authority.

Disciples were not just sent out to build a church. Christ sent them to exercise dominion. That is why the Jewish leaders got angry when the apostles came on the scene (see Acts 4). They couldn't keep these guys quiet. They jailed them and whipped them, but Peter and the others kept right on preaching Jesus. Later on, the Jews in Thessalonica said, "Uh-oh. Here come these men who have upset the whole world" (see Acts 17:6). The whole point of discipleship is that believers, and the church, share in Jesus' authority. Jesus' promise to be with us until the end of the age is specifically related to His personal presence as we make disciples.

What was it that gave the apostles the boldness to stand in the temple and preach right under the noses of the religious leaders who had the authority to flog, imprison, and even execute them? What had happened to change their lives so radically? The answer is back in Acts 2, in that upper room where Christ's followers were gathered together after His ascension into heaven. The answer came out of their own prolonged time for a collective solemn assembly. There were only 120 of them, but they were serious about Christ, about paying the price, about enduring the pain and inconvenience of being His kingdom disciples. God knew it, so He sent the Holy Spirit to indwell them just as He had promised. Those men and women, dedicated to Christ and filled with the Spirit, started making disciples in exactly the way Jesus told them to do.

Although 120 isn't a large number, there is a big lesson for us in that small figure. How often do we judge the importance of a church by the size of its membership? When we do that, we're missing the point. It's not how many members are in a church that matters—what counts is their faithfulness in making disciples of Christ.

The goal of discipleship is conformity to the Savior, being transformed into the image or likeness of Christ (see Rom. 8:29; 2 Cor. 3:17–18) in our character, conduct, attitudes, and actions—as well as in the exercise of His authority through us in the world.

A pastor friend of mine was visiting a college campus a number of years ago. He didn't know that my son Anthony Jr. was a student there. He said he was walking across campus and saw a young man off in the distance. My friend said he looked and then stopped dead in his tracks. "That has to be Tony Evans's son," he told himself. "He looks like Tony; he's built like Tony; he even walks like Tony."

He was right, of course. The young man he had spotted was Anthony. Even though the man was a long way away, Anthony's characteristics were so obviously like mine that my friend told me, "I didn't even know Anthony was in college yet. All I knew was that nobody could look that much like you and not be yours."

Let me tell you, people ought to be able to see you and your church from a long way off and say, "That person has to be a follower of Jesus Christ." They ought to be able to tell by the way you walk and talk—by the total orientation of your life—that you belong to Christ because nobody could function the way you function and not know Him. The family resemblance ought to be obvious. It ought to be clear where you and your church stand. That is kingdom discipleship.

CHAPTER FIVE

THE LEADERSHIP

◆

David shepherded Israel with integrity of heart. Yet, keep in mind, he also had skill of hand (see Ps. 78:72). An excellent leader must have both. This is because if you have heart without skill, you may love people and be a wonderful person yourself, but nothing will get done. Or if it gets done, it gets done poorly.

As leaders, we are not called to choose between the two. We are not called to have skill of hand without integrity of heart. Nor are we called to have integrity of heart without skill of hand. We are called to balance the two in order to create an atmosphere for a church ministry that does what it does well, yet all for the glory of God and the betterment of His children as well as the advancement of His kingdom. You, as a pastor and church leader, need both heart and hand if you are to lead well. The leaders you choose to serve under you need both as well.

So we need to find out what God wants the church's leaders to do because leadership is God's means of building His kingdom in history. Spiritual leadership demands the responsibility of advancing God's kingdom agenda by helping to facilitate the biblical goals of Christian maturity and ministry effectiveness in the lives of those who are under one's charge (see Eph. 4:11–12). Simply put, a leader is someone who knows the way, goes the way, and shows the way (see Ezra 7:10).

Spiritual leadership in the church is important for a number of reasons. First, it is important theologically because God is a God of order who works in history representatively (Ex. 18:13–27; 1 Cor. 11:3). Secondly, spiritual leadership is important ecclesiologically because the church is an institution that must be managed in an orderly fashion by qualified leadership (1 Tim. 3:1–13; Titus 1:5–9). Next, it is important anthropologically because people need and naturally look to other people for direction (Judg. 17:6; Num. 13–14). Likewise, spiritual leadership in the church is important spiritually because people need help in seeing and understanding how to live their lives from a divine framework rather than from a human perspective (James 3:1–18). Lastly, it is important culturally because the progress or regression of society is directly tied to divine sanctions operating in history (2 Chron. 15:3–6).

THE GOALS OF SPIRITUAL LEADERSHIP

The goal of spiritual leadership is discipleship, which we have seen is the developmental process of the local church. This process progressively brings Christians from spiritual infancy to spiritual maturity, so that they are then able to repeat the process with someone else (see Matt. 28:19–20). Discipleship does not occur at a point in time, rather it occurs over time. Church leaders are able to maximize the discipleship within the local church by increasing the opportunities for spiritual growth to occur (see 1 Cor. 2:15, 3:1–2; Heb. 5:12).

The goal of discipleship in the corporate body of local believers has not been fully completed until the disciple becomes a discipler, thus assuring the multiplication of God's people and the expansion of God's kingdom. We see this when Paul wrote to Timothy, "The things which you have heard from me in the presence of many witnesses, entrust these to faithful men *who will be able to teach others also*" (2 Tim. 2:2).

The Greek word translated as "men" in this passage is actually *anthrōpos* which refers to "a human being, whether male or female."[1] God expects the area of discipleship to be done *by* both men and women *for* both men and women.

A church will only be as strong as its leadership because God will not skip over the leaders and move to the congregation. But

---

1. "Anthrōpos," Strong's Concordance, Bible Hub, https://biblehub.com/greek/444.htm.

I'm not saying that God may not bless and develop the individual believers in a church even if the leaders are not all they are supposed to be. But a situation like that is comparable to a person who is in a miserable marriage. God can give that married person grace, but it's still going to be an unpleasant environment because God's appointed leader isn't leading well.

That's why the church is not just a place to become inspired by a sermon. It's a place where God's leaders oversee the process of discipleship so that His Word and His blessings may flow out to the congregation at large and disseminate from them out into the community and ultimately into the world.

The role of spiritual leadership is also to oversee the effective ministry organization (see 1 Tim. 3:15; Titus 1:5) and biblical proclamation of the local church for the advancement of God's kingdom agenda (see 1 Tim. 4:13; 2 Tim. 4:2; Titus 2:1). Spiritual leaders are critical because they are God's representatives, and throughout history God has always worked through the principle of representation. The principle of representation means that the person who has been placed over you can act for you. Within that "proxy," there can be great joy or great disaster, depending on the identity and effectiveness of your representative.

We see this principle at work with the first Adam bringing sin into the world and the second "Adam," Jesus Christ, bringing redemption through the cross. We can also see this principle at work in Genesis 18:16–33, where Abraham interceded for Sodom and Gomorrah. God told Abraham that if he could find ten people who were God's representatives in that wicked culture, He would change His mind about destroying Sodom and Gomorrah.

Let me show you how this principle of representation works today in the church. Paul wrote these words to Timothy, his spiritual son and disciple, who was pastoring in Ephesus:

> Until I come, give attention to the public reading of Scripture, to exhortation and teaching. Do not neglect the spiritual gift within you. . . . Take pains with these things; be absorbed in them, so that your progress will be evident to all. Pay close attention to yourself and to your teaching; persevere in these things, for as you do this you will ensure salvation both for yourself and for those who hear you. (1 Tim. 4:13–16)

Paul told Timothy that his ministry will determine not only his own spiritual fate but the fate of those in his congregation. In other words, Paul was speaking representatively. Timothy was God's representative leader to the saints at Ephesus.

Paul used the word "salvation" in verse 16 but not in the narrow sense of being born again. That was already true for Timothy and the believers at Ephesus. Paul was using this word in its broader sense of deliverance. Essentially, Paul told Timothy, "If you want to deliver yourself and your people and ensure God's blessing on the church, you must make sure you are functioning properly as God's representative through whom His blessings, power, and presence will flow."

The representative nature of God's work in history is a profound principle. It has enormous implications at every level of life, from our personal lives to our families and on to the church and the culture at large. As God's representatives, what we do as church leaders doesn't just impact us or the people to whom we minister; it has an impact on future generations and on the future of this nation and the world.

In 1 Peter 5, the apostle Peter wrote, "I exhort the elders among you, as your fellow elder and witness of the sufferings of Christ, and a partaker also of the glory that is to be revealed, shepherd the flock of God among you, exercising oversight" (vv. 1–2a). The Word of God calls a church congregation a "flock," and the leaders are to be its shepherds. Now you probably already know that calling someone a sheep is not a compliment. Sheep are easily led astray. In fact, if one sheep starts walking around in circles, another sheep will come follow it and start walking around in circles too. Another trait of sheep is their vulnerability. Sheep are an easy target for a predator. Once you become a member of God's flock, you become a target for the enemy's attack.

Before you came to Christ, you belonged in Satan's realm. So he didn't have to target you. He owned you. But when you came to Jesus Christ, you became Satan's target. Now he wants to keep you distracted from pursuing the advancement of God's kingdom on earth. That's why Paul told the elders at Miletus in Acts 20:28–29, "Be on guard for yourselves and for all the flock. . . . I know that after my departure savage wolves will come in among you, not sparing the flock."

Peter told church leaders to shepherd God's flock because they might not know when the wolves were out there. The elders didn't know that the particular circumstance or situation had been designed for their destruction. So Peter reminded them that as shepherds, they needed to watch for wolves who, as Jesus said, come in sheep's clothing (see Matt. 7:15).

Peter went on to tell leaders to shepherd the flock of God "not under compulsion, but voluntarily, according to the will of God; and not for sordid gain, but with eagerness; nor yet as lording it over those allotted to your charge, but proving to be examples to the flock" (vv. 2b–3). True leaders serve with an eagerness and commitment that comes from knowing they are doing God's will as well as from a heart that truly cares for the well-being of those being served. True leaders are humble and others-centered.

Leaders exist to protect and preserve the sheep, not lead them astray. God calls leaders to shepherd His flock because sheep are prone to wander and are vulnerable to attack. Leaders also serve as role models, illustrating in their lives what they teach so that the flock can follow not only their words but also their actions (see 1 Tim. 4:12).

THE CATEGORIES
OF CHURCH LEADERSHIP

Scripture identifies three distinct leadership roles for the church: pastor, elder, and deacon. The **pastor**, or pastor-teacher as described by Paul in Ephesians 4:11, is the church's spiritual leader. In a multiple staff church, the senior pastor is charged with the primary responsibility for the church's spiritual health and direction. I would summarize the pastor's role as proclaiming the Word and overseeing the work, which includes developing leaders who are qualified to serve as elders and deacons.

Make no mistake about it, no matter how big a church's staff may be, there is (formally or informally) always a primary leader who has been invested by God with vision, authority, and responsibility. This leader is accountable to the body of elders (see 1 Tim. 5:17). The church's leadership does not rest in committees. There has to be a place where final decisions are made and there has to be a leader who leads the way in formulating and implementing the church's vision. God always transfers leadership to a person, whether it be from Moses to Joshua, Elijah to Elisha, or Paul to Timothy. God places His vision in the hands of a person.

The second New Testament classification of leaders is the **elders**. These are the spiritually qualified men who form the governing body of the church and in whose hands the confirmation of the final policy decisions rest. The pastor is an elder also, for Paul talked about elders "who work hard at preaching and teaching" (1 Tim. 5:17).

The Bible also teaches that elders must be spiritual men. "If any man aspires to the office of overseer, it is a fine work he desires to do" (1 Tim. 3:1). The word for *man* is the gender specific word for males. The principle of male leadership in the church is established earlier in 1 Timothy: "I do not allow a woman to teach or exercise authority over a man" (2:12). Paul's statement in 1 Corinthians 14:34–35 that women are to be silent in church doesn't mean they can't speak. The issue there is exercising final authority.

Let me add that I am not talking about spiritual gifts here, but the *office* of elder. Women in the church are very gifted, even more so than men in many cases. And God allows women to use their gifts in the church. In fact, the Scripture allows women to do anything in church except be an elder or a senior pastor. In God's divine sovereignty, He has determined that final leadership in the church is restricted to men.

The clear pattern in Scripture is a plurality of elders in each church. For example, Acts 14:23 says that Paul and his missionary team appointed "elders [plural] for them in every church [singular]." James tells us that if anyone is sick, he should "call for the elders of the church" (James 5:14), the same pattern as in Acts. Paul left Titus in Crete to "appoint elders in every city" (Titus 1:5). Timothy's spiritual gift was bestowed by "the presbytery," or the governing board of the church at Ephesus (1 Tim. 4:14).

Lastly, let's look at the office of **deacon**. The Greek word for deacon means "servant." This office is interesting because nowhere in Scripture do we find a deacon board. There is the elder board but no corresponding formal organization of deacons. This is because the deacons only have one basic job, which is to execute the church policies and ministries that have been established by the elders and the pastor or staff of pastors, which includes a senior pastor and associate pastors.

Deacons are to do more than serve communion and count the offerings. They must be spiritually mature and responsible men and women. Yes, Scripture states that women can be deacons because of 1 Timothy 3:11, which says, "Women must likewise be dignified, not malicious gossips, but temperate, faithful in all things." In the context, Paul is talking about women who serve as deacons, since he mentions deacons' wives separately in verse 12.

Paul used the word *women* here because there is no Greek word for "deaconess." These women are clearly distinguished from deacons' wives. He was not saying that only men can be deacons, but that those men who are selected be faithful to their wives. If verse 11 is only talking about deacons' wives, we have a problem because that means Paul skipped over the qualifications for elders' wives. This would have made deacons' wives more important and under closer scrutiny than the wives of elders. So it is clear to me that Paul was talking about deaconesses, or women who function on an equal level with male deacons. Paul called Phoebe "a servant," the same word for deacon (Rom. 16:1).

The job of deacons is to fan out among the flock to make sure that the ministry gets done and the saints are cared for. They are the church's foot soldiers. Deacons are accountable to the elders, but the biblical pattern indicates that deacons do not come together as a separate governing board.

CHAPTER SIX

THE MEMBERSHIP

◆

Believers are knit together in a bond of family that is critical to the church's function. The church is to be that place where no one stands alone. A Christian without a church home is like an organ without a body, a sheep without a flock, or a child without a family. This is why God calls the local church a family (Eph. 2:19).

"I don't have to go to church to be saved. I don't have to belong to a church to be a Christian. I can worship God in my home." Have you ever heard this given as an excuse from people who do not want to go to, or be a functioning part of, a local church? It's sometimes difficult to refute because it happens to be true, to a point. Nothing you do and nothing you can join makes you a Christian.

THE VALUE

So what then is the value of the church? Do Christians have a mandate for membership? To find the answers to these questions, I want us to look at the book of Hebrews—an epistle written to a group of Jewish believers on the verge of defecting from the faith in the face of severe persecution. The writer of Hebrews states,

> Let us draw near to God with a sincere heart and with the full assurance that faith brings, having our hearts sprinkled to cleanse us from a guilty conscience and having our bodies washed with pure water. Let us hold unswervingly to the hope we profess, for he who promised is faithful. And let us consider how we may spur one another on toward love and good deeds, not giving up meeting together, as some are in the habit of doing, but encouraging one another—and all the more as you see the Day approaching. (Heb. 10:22–25 NIV)

The book of Hebrews is probably second only to Revelation on the list of *Most Difficult Biblical Books To Understand*. Making complete sense of it requires a thorough comprehension of Old Testament customs and theology, most notably the concept of *covenant*. By definition, a covenant is *a divinely established, spiritually binding relationship between two or more parties who agree to function under a designated structure of authority in accordance with revealed guidelines resulting in long-term effects.*

For the purpose of our discussion, let's focus specifically on how this covenant relationship with God is established. In Old Testament times, the blood of sacrificed animals, offered in accordance with laws and customs laid out by God, temporarily washed the sins of mankind away.

When Jesus gave His life on the cross, He became the "mediator of a new covenant" (Heb. 9:15) in which our sins were cleansed not by the blood of bulls, goats, and sheep but by the sacrifice of the Savior. The church then is the "community of the covenant"—the assembly of those who share in the sacrifice of God's Son.

It's important to understand that it is within the context of this covenant community that many of the benefits of our relationship with Christ are realized. In the same way that children are promised a greater length and quality of life if they keep covenant with their parents through obedience (see Eph. 6:1–3) and in the same way a husband is provided access to God in prayer based on his relationship with his wife (see 1 Peter 3:7), so some of the advantages individual Christians enjoy can only be experienced as they relate properly to the family of God in the context of the local church. Unfortunately, too many Christians are spiritual orphans with no family or like foster children bouncing around from place to place, never landing anywhere.

For example, Paul tells us that Christians can only experience the spiritual growth they need as they are linked with other believers (Eph. 4:12–16). God shows His supernatural power in meeting the needs of His people as the church brings Him glory (Eph. 3:20–21). On the other side of the coin, God promises to judge those who bring harm to the church (1 Cor. 3:16–18). There is a level of personal care and support that can only be realized in the dynamic relationship of the local church (1 Cor. 12:18–20, 25), which is to function like a human body. This can only occur through formal, accountable connectivity. God's power over Satan can only be fully experienced in the context of the covenant of the church (Eph. 3:10).

Here's the point: our relationship to the corporate body of Christians is crucial to our personal relationship with God (see 1 John 4:12). Church membership may be properly defined as *the commitment to be identified and dynamically involved with a local body of believers who are growing together as disciples of Jesus Christ.* Just as believers share a formal and relational connection with Christ in conversion and just as the members of our physical bodies have a formal and functional attachment, even so Christians are to have a formal and functional relationship to a local body of believers.

Our commitment is not only to Christ but to other Christians as well (see 2 Cor. 8:5). In fact, our fellowship with other Christians can actually validate or invalidate our fellowship with Christ (see 1 John 2:19). While our salvation is personal, it is not private. If all of us in the body don't play the part God has called us to play, then the ministry of the church will be stymied. And to the degree that we stymie the church, accordingly we will lose God's blessing and incur His judgment (see 1 Cor. 3:16–17).

Paul said something profoundly important about Christ's body, the church, in 1 Corinthians 12: "If one member suffers, all the members suffer with it; if one member is honored, all the members rejoice with it" (v. 26). I can't emphasize often enough that we as Christians are joined together in a vital, living, organic unity that is indispensable to the church's proper functioning and its impact in the world.

Membership in a local church is necessary for a believer to partake consistently of the four vital experiences of worship, fellowship, education, and outreach that are necessary for the discipleship process to occur. No church membership means limited or no discipleship and is outright rebellion against the expressed will of God.

When Jesus gave His life on the cross, He became "the mediator of a new covenant" (Heb. 9:15) in which our sins were cleansed by His sacrifice. The church, then, is the "community of the covenant," the assembly of those who share in the sacrifice of God's Son, and thus tap into the benefits of the covenant collectively on a greater level.

Believers are to use their God-given gifts within the context of the local church to build up the body of Christ and serve the kingdom of God. Ephesians 4 is a classic passage that makes this absolutely clear. Paul wrote, "And [Christ] gave some as . . . pastors and teachers, for the equipping of the saints for the work of service, to the building up of the body of Christ" (vv. 11–12).

There is no such thing as a Christian who does not serve the kingdom by ministering to the church. You can't build a home without all the members doing their part, and you can't build a church without all the members doing their part. Therefore, pastors need to make sure that their congregation understands the importance of having a functional church membership, not merely church attenders. Membership means more than people just attending worship services.

Paul went on to say:

> We are to grow up in all aspects into Him who is the head, even Christ, from whom the whole body, being fitted and held together by what every joint supplies, according to the proper working of each individual part, causes the growth of the body for the building up of itself in love. (Eph. 4:15–16)

Every member of the body has a part to play in making the body function. Your job as a church leader is not to do the ministry while the people watch. That's why I believe it is a sin for a person to benefit from the ministry of the church and yet not contribute anything. Too many people come to church and say, "Preach to me. Sing to me. Serve me. If I'm sick, visit me. If I'm hurting, comfort me. If I need encouragement, encourage me. But don't expect me to give any of my time, talents, or resources to this work."

Such a member is a church leech and not a truly functioning church member, sucking the lifeblood of the church's ministry without making any meaningful contribution. That's a sin and an insult to the Father who has invited us into His family. We are not in His family because we deserve to be here. We are here by grace (Eph. 2:8–9), adopted into God's family, and therefore should consider it a privilege to serve the Lord and our spiritual brothers and sisters.

God did not call 20 percent of the church to serve the other 80 percent. He called 100 percent of us to serve each other. That's why at our church in Dallas, people must agree to serve in one of the many ministry opportunities offered before they are accepted into the membership. As we saw earlier in David's leadership combination of heart and skill, members also need to engage with each other and serve one another with both heart and skill. Therefore, the pastor should make sure that the church is offering meaningful opportunities for members to utilize their spiritual gifts for the building up of the body, as well as ministry to the community under the guidance and accountability of loving, spiritual leaders. Remember, the church grows through what every joint supplies (see Eph. 4:16).

Across the street from our church in Dallas is our Education Center, which gives us the space and technology to hold a huge variety of programs—particularly for children and youth—but also supplemented with many adult programs. Some time ago, however, we encountered a major problem in this center. People entering on the east side of the building were being hit with a putrid smell, and they quickly let us know that something was wrong. So we had this dilemma that despite the size and cost of this building, and despite all the programs that were held there, the environment was not conducive to accomplishing the purposes for which the building had been built.

We brought in professionals to try to find out why such a valuable facility was also such an offensive one. They discovered that a pipe coming off one of the restrooms was cracked and leaking. At the same time, the fan designed to vent the bathroom was actually turning the wrong way, pushing the odor back down into the building instead of lifting it out. Until the problem was fixed and the atmosphere was cleared, a facility that was designed for good was being contaminated by something bad.

There's a lesson here for us as pastors and leaders of churches. If there is a contaminated atmosphere in your church membership caused by a faulty spiritual, relational, or emotional connection among the members, it doesn't matter how much money you spend on plans and programs or how carefully your calendar is laid out. It doesn't even matter how great you preach. Until the reason for the "odor" is addressed, what was designed for good will become contaminated.

LOVING ONE ANOTHER

God created the church to be an environment where healthy spiritual relationships are fostered and where authentic Christianity is lived out. However, far too often the church has become a place of unwanted odors. These stem from unhealthy relationships, selfishness, laziness, legalism and more. Many, if not most, of the issues we face in our churches stem from disobedience to God's commands for "one another," particularly the command to love one another (1 John 4:21). Were we to love each other in the manner that God has instructed us, then our relationships, small groups, congregations, and church leadership teams would be pleasing to all of us.

God wants the church to be a community where real people in real relationships are meeting real needs in real ways. God did not create the church simply as a classroom where you give or get instruction, or as a theater where performances are put on for entertainment.

Too often we in the church are like those cutout figures you find at a carnival. There is the body of a beauty queen or a muscleman with the face cut out so people can stick their heads in and have their picture taken while pretending to be that person. But it doesn't take a genius to see that the face and the body don't go together. We can run into that problem spiritually. Jesus is the head of the body, which is His church. But too often the head and the body don't look like they belong together. The apostle Paul has an answer for that problem in Romans 12:9–13.

Paul begins this section by saying: "Let love be without hypocrisy. Abhor what is evil; cling to what is good" (v. 9). True biblical love is *compassionately and righteously pursuing the well-being of another.* Now I added the word "true" because Paul basically says, "Don't love with a mask on." In other words, don't just play the part.

The word translated "hypocrite" comes from the ancient Greek theater. There weren't enough actors to play all the parts, so the actors would play multiple characters by holding a mask over their faces. Those actors were called hypocrites, so you can see how this word came to mean someone who isn't sincere but is simply pretending. We say they are wearing a mask. The tragedy is that some of the best actors and actresses you'll ever see are in church, because they come with a mask on.

Here's the problem with wearing the mask: when we are

not real with God, ourselves, and others, when we are trying to hide who we are, we are operating in the dark. Now the Bible says, "God is Light, and in Him there is no darkness at all" (1 John 1:5). Then John goes on to say in verse 6, "If we say that we have fellowship with Him and yet walk in the darkness, we lie and do not practice the truth." Light exposes while darkness conceals, so when we are operating in the dark, we wind up lying to God, to ourselves, and to others.

But the biblical standard for Christians is love without hypocrisy—no masks. Paul continued in Romans 12:9 to give two boundaries to this love: "Abhor what is evil; cling to what is good." It calls wrong, wrong and right, right because love doesn't negate the truth. The body of Christ ought to be an environment where you and I can love and be loved without wearing a mask or feeling the need to "perform" our Christianity because we are in an authentic environment for truth.

Paul continues his admonition in Romans 12 by saying, "Be devoted to one another in brotherly love; give preference to one another in honor." The word "brotherly love" deals with love in the context of a family. The word "devoted" means to be committed to one another. This is not a word of casual relationships. There is no thought in the Bible of the church as a place of casual contact and casual relationships. No, Paul says the church is to be a place where we are devoted to each other in love. God wants us as His children to be devoted to one another so we can benefit one another.

If I were to paraphrase what Paul is saying in Romans 12:10, it would go like this: "I want you to be searching for opportunities to impact somebody outside of yourself." If we fail to love one another horizontally in carrying out God's commands and precepts for "one another," we are not going to experience all of God's vertical working in our lives. A lot of Christians are hindering the flow of God's blessing by being focused only on themselves. There must be an outward (horizontal) focus to our lives in order to fully manifest the upward (vertical) experience of God.

Your members need to understand that to join a church is not merely to have a place to sit on Sunday. It is to build community with other believers. This is what God is after, and when the church becomes authentic, it creates a healthy environment in which God is free to move.

GOD'S "BRAND"

Designers and product manufacturers are known by their brands. Trademarks, logos, and branding in general distinguish a company, person, or platform in such a way that uniquely separates it from any other. It sets the stage for expectations on deliverables. It communicates values, atmosphere, and intention. It goes much further than broadcasting identification and purpose by placing that identity and purpose within the backdrop of how they connect with the larger whole of life in general.

Pastors, God's "brand" isn't people carrying the Bible underneath their arms. Nor is it the use of "Christianese," language designed to make someone sound more holy or spiritual than others. It isn't even showing up for church service on Sundays or Wednesdays. God's brand is more innately ingrained in the very fabric of life.

To know God's brand is to know His heart and His character. To reflect His brand is to reflect Christ Himself. Jesus told us what God's brand is—the overarching, dominating trait we are to be known for—when He gathered His disciples in an upper room to give them His final message prior to His death, resurrection, and ascension in Luke 22:14–27 and John 13:1–32. In that room, He told them the identifying factor of belonging to Him as His follower is through serving others in such a way that it brings glory to God.

We read about this in John 13:31–32, where Jesus uses the word "glory," or a form of it, five times. As you know, glory means *to advertise or show off something.* It means to embellish it or put it on display. In these two verses, Jesus mentions this concept repetitively giving us a visual of how the Son glorifies the Father and how the Father glorifies the Son. In essence, they are each advertising the other, like a billboard reflecting the goodness in the other.

As Jesus continues His discourse with His friends and followers, we discover that we have also been called to be a part of putting this glory on display, similar to God's own advertising agency. You and I have been called to glorify God, as well as Jesus Christ, through our lives, and we do this by reflecting His brand. Jesus says,

> "Little children, I am with you a little while longer. You will seek Me; and as I said to the Jews, now I also say to you, 'Where I am going, you cannot come.' A new commandment I give to you, that you *love one another*, even as I have loved you, that you also *love one another*. By this all men will know that you are My disciples, if you have *love for one another*." (vv. 33–35)

Three times in this passage Jesus tells us we are to love others. So the question we need to answer today is what is love, and how do we do it? The biblical definition of the Greek word for love, *agape*, is *the decision to compassionately, responsibly, and righteously pursue the well being of another*. It is setting someone else's needs and betterment higher than they may even set them for themselves. It doesn't equate to liking someone. In fact, you can love people that you don't even like because love is an intentional choice to do good for another.

Jesus distinguishes love from just an emotional feeling

when He says, "A new commandment I give you . . ." Jesus specifically uses the word "commandment" in relationship to love. We can rarely command our feelings to do anything at all. But we can always command our actions through the power of our mind and our will enabled by the Holy Spirit.

Biblical love involves a decision, whether or not it is accompanied by emotion. It is a decision to compassionately, responsibly, and righteously pursue the betterment of another person. Which is why you can even love your enemies according to Christ's command (see Matt. 5:44).

We read in Romans, "But God demonstrates His own love toward us, in that while we were yet sinners, Christ died for us" (5:8). God showed us the actions of love when we were unlovable. When we were annoying, irregular, unlikeable, and unpredictable, God demonstrated His love for us in giving up the greatest sacrifice, His Son Jesus Christ, on our behalf. That is the truest revelation of love: doing something on someone's behalf that they cannot do for themselves, especially when they do not even ask you or thank you at the time. God has modeled perfect love for us so that we can understand and reflect His love for others.

One of the main reasons the enemy seeks to bring about division in the body of Christ is because it is a direct opposite to Christ's command to love. Where there are divisions, God is not being glorified. Satan doesn't want us to be effective at advertising the glory of God or manifesting His brand of love to those around us, so he'll use racial, personality, class divisions, and more to keep us apart.

Loving one another is not just a commandment carrying no benefits. Love taps into the very core of God's nature (see 1 John 4:8) and through obedience, we can experience the presence, love, peace, and power of God in our lives as pastors and in the lives of your members.

CHAPTER SEVEN

THE DISTINCTIVES

◆

All of us are familiar with the story of Humpty Dumpty, the figure from the children's nursery rhyme whose world was shattered after he had a great fall. He called on the best his world had to offer to address his problem—"all the king's horses and all the king's men." We would say today that Humpty had the White House, the Congress, the military, and any other human power or authority you can think of coming to his aid in brokenness.

But the tragedy of the story is that none of these human powers could put Humpty Dumpty's life and world back together again. Apparently, Mr. Dumpty had no biblically functioning church available to help him because if he had, he would not have had to call on the king in the first place.

Now it's one thing when a nursery rhyme character cannot

find the help he needs to repair his shattered world, even when his problem is being attended to by the highest authorities the culture has to offer. But it's another thing altogether when real people in the real world discover that all the human institutions of power and influence can't fix society's deepest problems or address people's deepest needs.

This is where the church comes in because the church is the most important institution on earth. The church, and only the church, has been commissioned by the sovereign Lord to be His representative agency in history. It has been given sole authority to unlock the treasures of the spiritual realm so that they can be brought to bear on the realities of earth. The church alone possesses the keys to the kingdom.

Thus, as the church goes, so goes everything else. God designed the church to be the epicenter of culture, and the church's strength or weakness is a major determining factor in the success or failure of human civilization. When the church is strong, the culture is impacted positively—even if the "powers that be" in a particular place don't realize that impact and seek to marginalize and persecute the church. But when the church is weak, its influence deteriorates and so does the culture.

SPIRITUAL MISSION OF THE CHURCH

It is important to understand the church's importance for cultural reasons, since Jesus called His people to be salt and light, a city on a hill. But understanding the church's nature and mission is even more important for spiritual reasons. That's because the church has been given the assignment of growing all of its members into mature believers who can disciple others and maximize their spiritual potential.

Second Chronicles 15:3–6 sets the scene for us to explore the centrality of the church by showing what happens when the church (God's collective, chosen people) fails at its mission. The prophet Azariah was urging King Asa of Judah to continue the reforms he had begun. To reinforce his message, Azariah reminded Asa of the sad condition God's people were in during an earlier age, which many Bible commentators believe was the period of the judges. If so, Azariah was speaking of Israel's low point spiritually when he said, "For many days Israel was without the true God and without a teaching priest and without law" (v 3).

Verse 4 refers to those times when Israel sought God during that period, but in verses 5–6, the prophet summarized those days of chaos and God's judgment:

> In those times there was no peace to him who went out or to him who came in, for many disturbances afflicted all the inhabitants of the lands. Nation was crushed by nation, and city by city, for God troubled them with every kind of distress.

Several things from these verses are worth noting. For instance, the description of a society in the grip of violence, crime, and conflict between nations sounds like our world today, so we know there's a lesson for us here. Like the world of ancient Israel, our culture is also in chaos and confusion.

But what ought to grab your attention is the statement in verse 6 that this all came about because "God troubled" the people. We might have expected Azariah to say that this mess was the result of satanic activity and influence in the world. According to the prophet, however, God was the author of this confusion among the people, although He was not in any way the author of their sin that provoked His judgment.

In other words, these problems that were tearing apart the fabric of society had a spiritual cause. So to address the lack of peace on a social level, try to deal with violence and crime through more law enforcement, or settle conflicts between governments at the bargaining table would not be sufficient because the people's problem was with God. And when God is your problem, only God is your solution.

What was it about this period of Israel's history that caused God to "trouble" His people with distress at so many levels? The root of the problem is found in 2 Chronicles 15:3. Three key elements that are necessary to keep God's people on track spiritually were missing.

The first of these elements was *the lack of "the true God."* This does not say that God had withdrawn Himself from Israel so that the people forgot who He was or could no longer find Him. Even in the days of the judges, there was religious service going on in Israel. People were offering sacrifices to God. But it was not the kind of authentic religion that pleased God.

We could say that the Israelites had forgotten the kind of holy God they were serving, so they thought nothing of going off into idolatry or mixing with pagans or violating His law in a dozen other ways. Israel was living as if it couldn't tell the one true God from the many false gods around it. Spiritual activity was going on, but it wasn't true to God's requirements.

What could have caused God's people to get all confused about the nature of God and start mixing the true with the false? In the case before us, the second phrase of 2 Chronicles 15:3 gives us a large clue: Israel lacked "a teaching priest." We would say today that the nation had a very serious pastoral problem—a mist in the pulpit that became a fog in the pew.

Notice that the text does not say that Israel had no priests. The problem was that the priests were not carrying out their function of teaching God's law so the people would know the true God and what He expected of them. The priests were doing an inadequate job of providing a kingdom viewpoint through which the people could interpret all of life and make God-honoring decisions.

Now don't misunderstand. People are responsible for their own relationship to God and their obedience to His revealed will, especially in a day like today when we each have a copy of God's Word and the ability to read it. But I'm talking about a systemic spiritual failure at the heart of Israel's spiritual leadership that kept the people uninformed and ill-informed about their responsibility before God and the consequences of failing to meet it. In short, the leaders were not developing kingdom disciples.

The third problem mentioned in 2 Chronicles 15:3 follows as a natural consequence of the first two. Because the people didn't know their God intimately and were not hearing His Word taught, they were "without law." That is, they didn't know how to apply God's law to the situations they faced. The divine rules weren't being applied, so people made up their own.

The very end of the book of Judges illustrates this problem perfectly: "Everyone did what was right in his own eyes" (Judg. 21:25). Everybody had an idea of what to do, but nothing worked because God's government of His people was not being upheld and enforced. The commitment to conforming to an absolute objective standard of truth had been lost. The people of Israel didn't know how to bring God's truth to bear on their world, and the practical result was that they lived as if no divine framework existed at all.

Look at our nation today. How can we have all of these churches on every corner with all of these preachers and programs and facilities, and yet still have such moral and spiritual chaos in our culture? It's because we, as God's pastors and church leaders, aren't bringing His Word and His power to bear in the churches we lead or on the world around us, so people are living as if God doesn't exist.

Since the basic realities of spiritual conflict and the superior power of the spiritual world haven't changed since the days of the judges in ancient Israel, we see the same principle of the visible world being controlled by the invisible world at work today. Paul gave us one of the clearest statements of this reality in Ephesians 6:12 when he said, "Our struggle is not against flesh and blood, but against the rulers, against the powers, against the world forces of this darkness, against the spiritual forces of wickedness in the heavenly places."

This is also a great statement of why the church is central to God's plan. God has always had a vehicle or an agency on earth to make His presence manifest, carry out His will, and bring what is invisible and spiritual down to the world of the visible and the physical.

Israel's system of the law, the sacrifices, and the priesthood was God's agency to accomplish His program on earth in the Old Testament. Today that agency is the church and only the church. The centrality of the church cannot be overstated. Now that doesn't mean God cannot reveal Himself to someone apart from the visible presence of a church. But the Bible is clear that the church is the entity that brings the realm of heaven into history and brings the values of heaven to bear on earth.

THE ANGELIC CONFLICT

Pastor, your understanding of the angelic conflict is crucial to having a proper view of the church you lead and our place as pastors in God's plan. I'm going to summarize a lot of biblical material that you can read on your own. Two key passages you'll want to review are Isaiah 14:12–14 and Ezekiel 28:11–19. Some scholars believe these passages reference a historical figure of that time, but I believe these passages describe an angelic being named Lucifer so beautiful and so awe-inspiring that he stood next to the very throne of God and directed the myriads of other angels in worshiping God. His name means "light-bearer," and he is called "star of the morning, son of the dawn" (Isa. 14:12).

We know that the angels are eternal spirit beings created by God to carry out His will and give Him the glory and the worship that He is due. The angels themselves are glorious creatures, and Lucifer was the most glorious of all. He was at the top of the angelic hierarchy. The description of him in Ezekiel 28 is nothing short of spectacular.

But at some point, Lucifer fell in love with himself and decided he was tired of worshiping God. The Bible says of Lucifer, "Your heart was lifted up because of your beauty; you corrupted your wisdom by reason of your splendor" (Ezek. 28:17). Lucifer wanted to be worshiped as God, and he convinced one-third of the angels to follow him in open rebellion against God's throne (see Rev. 12:4). Lucifer's arrogance is summarized in the five times he declared, "I will," culminating in the boast "I will make myself like the Most High" (Isa. 14:13–14).

But God uncovered Lucifer's rebellion and put him and the angels who followed him on trial for treason. The rebels led by Lucifer were found guilty and sentenced to eternal punishment. (Jesus said in Matthew 25:41 that hell was first prepared for the devil and his angels.) God also changed Lucifer's name to Satan, the "adversary." He became the enemy of God.

But instead of immediately throwing Satan and his demons into hell, the Bible says that the devil was "cut down to the earth" (Isa. 14:12). God banished the devil and his followers to a small speck of creation called earth. There the devil would enter into a conflict with another part of God's creation, mankind, and in the process God would be vindicated and glorified, and His power would be displayed, in an amazing way.

Why did God allow Satan to set up operations on earth and wreak his havoc? The best explanation is a theological one. That is, the Godhead conferred in Trinitarian session and decreed that Satan's rebellion and judgment would be used as an opportunity to demonstrate God's power, glory, justice, and righteousness—not only to Satan and his demons themselves, but to all of creation including mankind.

To appreciate the importance of this, you have to understand what a heinous, wicked act Satan's rebellion was. Here was the most beautiful and powerful of all God's creatures, not only rising up and shaking his fist in the face of the almighty, eternal God, but dragging one-third of God's holy angels with him—and doing so in God's perfect heaven! This was defiance, hatred, and ingratitude of monumental proportions.

Sin of this magnitude demanded more than judgment. The sinners needed to be made an example so others would see and understand and know better than to try to rebel against God. In fact, in order to demonstrate their divine power, glory, and wisdom the Godhead decided to use a creature that was far below the angels in stature to demonstrate what God can do with a lesser being who will love and obey and depend on Him—all those things that mighty Lucifer and his angelic followers refused to do.

Who is this lesser creature? Enter mankind. Hebrews 2:7 says we were created "for a little while lower than the angels." God made us this way to demonstrate to all of creation that when weak and powerless creatures like us yield ourselves to Him, neither Satan nor the demons can overpower us.

But in order to showcase His power and glory, God had to allow Satan access to us human beings so that He could prove once for all that "greater is He who is in [us] than he who is in the world" (1 John 4:4). When Satan gained access to the heart and mind of Eve and then Adam, the conflict began. But the good news is that God limited Satan's power to that of an influencer. That is, he can tempt and try to deceive, but he cannot overpower people against their will, and he is ultimately a defeated foe because of Christ.

So whenever a person is saved, the power and glory of God are on display for heaven and earth to see. Whenever a believer resists Satan's temptations and lives in victory, God's righteousness and holiness are revealed. And by the way, this issue of the angelic conflict is so important to God that when He got ready to deal Satan the decisive defeat, He didn't hurl a lightning bolt from heaven or simply crush Satan with a word. Instead, He sent His Son in the very form of that lesser creature to whip Satan face to face in the wilderness and for good on the cross. John wrote, "The Son of God appeared for this purpose, to destroy the works of the devil" (1 John 3:8).

God created the church to be His agency in this age representing His bigger plan, which is the kingdom. Satan knows this, which is why he works so hard to keep churches divided. He knows that whenever God's people really get together, his influence is severely limited.

Alexander the Great conquered the world for the Greek empire, but within a few years of his death, his kingdom was split among four of his generals. Even though the Roman Empire lasted for several hundred years, it is long gone and forgotten except in the history books. But the church is still seeking, however imperfectly, to obey the purpose for which our Founder, Jesus Christ, established it.

Jesus made a very important declaration to His disciples the night before He was crucified. As they reclined at the Last Supper, Jesus said, "Truly, truly, I say to you, he who believes in Me, the works that I do, he will do also; and greater works than these he will do; because I go to the Father" (John 14:12). We are certainly not greater than our Lord, but we can do greater things than He did in terms of our wide impact because the church has taken the gospel around the world and has brought countless numbers of people to faith in Christ. We are also able to do greater works because the Holy Spirit has come to indwell and empower each believer. This could not happen until Jesus returned to His Father (see John 16:7).

During the Spanish Civil War, a communist general coined the term "fifth column" to refer to people working within a society to subvert it on behalf of their cause. This general said he had four columns of troops marching on Madrid, and a fifth column already in the city doing whatever it took to help topple the existing government. The term "fifth column" became a popular way to describe people who infiltrate a society, using every means at their disposal to bring down the culture for the benefit of the invading army.

The church is Jesus' "fifth column." Believers are to see themselves as emissaries of God's kingdom invading the society around them to bring people under the obedience and rule of Jesus Christ. The problem we have is too many people are running around aimlessly in the church because they have never understood the church's true purpose.

According to Ephesians 3, the church is the culmination of God's plan for the ages that will demonstrate to the entire angelic realm His infinite wisdom in choosing weak vessels like us through whom to manifest His glory. In Ephesians 3:9, Paul was explaining to the Ephesians his ministry as the one whom God called to reveal the mystery of the church—a mystery that had been "hidden" for ages, but was now being revealed with the intent that "the manifold wisdom of God might now be made known through the church to the rulers and the authorities in the heavenly places" (v. 10).

The mention of "heavenly places" highlights the angelic conflict and God's plan to accomplish His will through mankind. These "rulers and authorities" are angelic beings, which includes both the holy angels who serve God and Satan and his demons as they work through human agents. Remember that God wanted to demonstrate what He could do with a lesser creature who would obey and follow Him.

You need to understand that this plan God set in motion to redeem fallen humanity and call out a people for His name, culminating in the church, was all a big surprise to Satan. He must have thought he outwitted God when he deceived Adam and Eve and plunged the race into sin. But Satan didn't understand what Christ was going to achieve on the cross. The devil wanted to destroy Jesus, but he didn't count on the resurrection. Paul said if the "rulers of this age" understood what God was really up to, they would not have crucified Christ (1 Cor. 2:8). The church is God's way of saying to the angelic realm, "This is the plan and purpose I have been carrying out on earth."

The church not only reveals to Satan and his demons how God has defeated them in Christ, but we are also the revelation of God's plan to the angels. Peter said the angels wanted to know more about God's plan of salvation and were very curious to look into it (see 1 Peter 1:12). This is an awesome truth in itself, but it gets better. The church is not just a demonstration piece to the angelic realm. God has given us the ability to impact and stir up this realm. That's what spiritual warfare is all about. We have the Spirit and the armor of God to defeat Satan at every turn.

That takes care of the demonic world, but how does the church move the angels to action? We do so by operating under the authority God has established. There's an example of this in 1 Corinthians 11:10, where we are told that when a woman is in church, "[she] ought to have a symbol of authority on her head, because of the angels." This symbol is a head covering that demonstrates that the woman accepts the authority of her husband and is operating in alignment with God.

How can this submission to authority affect the angels? Because the angels only operate under authority themselves.

Jude said that even the great archangel Michael did not try to usurp the devil's realm of authority as they disputed over Moses' body (see Jude 9). To do so would have been to violate the angelic chain of authority. In other words, the angels respond when we are functioning within God's established chain of authority. God sends the angels into action on our behalf when we are operating in obedience to Him and within His established lines of authority.

This is an awesome thought. Today, the church can get the holy angels active in history and stop Satan and the demonic world from wreaking their havoc. And by the way, just so you won't think this is all theoretical, read Acts 12 and the story of Peter's release from prison by an angel in response to the prayers of the church in Jerusalem.

It's no wonder that Paul concluded Ephesians 3 with a doxology: "Now to Him who is able to do far more abundantly beyond all that we ask or think, according to the power that works within us, to Him be the glory in the church and in Christ Jesus to all generations forever and ever. Amen" (vv. 20–21). The church is to live for God's glory, and one way we glorify Him is to manifest His wisdom and power to the angelic realm while actually influencing that realm by our obedience to God.

THE COMPLETION
OF CHRIST'S PROGRAM ON EARTH

Here's another facet of the church's distinctives: the church is to complete Christ's program by which His eternal plan is carried out in history. Ephesians 4:7–16 is a powerful passage that teaches that *every believer is gifted for service* and that *Christ has also given the church gifted people to lead it.* The Bible says, "To each one of us grace was given according to the measure of Christ's gift" (v. 7).

Paul used an Old Testament quotation to describe the Lord's activity prior to His ascension: "When He ascended on high, He led captive a host of captives, and He gave gifts to men" (v. 8). Then verses 9–10 are added as a parenthesis explaining what Paul meant by this intriguing statement.

In the process of completing His triumph over sin and death, Jesus was authorized by the Father to hand out gifts. This is a very picturesque phrase, which was used of a Roman general who defeated his enemy and brought back the spoils of the conquered kingdom to be used for the benefit of his own land. Jesus so completely defeated Satan by His death on the cross that He was able to march into Satan's own domain and rob him of his influence and use of a large portion of unredeemed humanity when they transferred from Satan's use to Christ's kingdom and His service as they were saved, thus also using their spiritual gifts for the glory of God.

This gifting also includes gifted leaders for the church (see Eph. 4:11). These leaders, including you as a pastor, have this assignment: "The equipping of the saints for the work of service, to the building up of the body of Christ" (v. 12). The church does not pay pastors to do all of the church's work, but to prepare the members of the body for their ministry.

No other organization except the church has been called into being by God Himself through the supernatural ministry of the Holy Spirit and charged with the specific task of carrying out Christ's work here on earth. Several more of the church's important distinctives are found in a key passage that Paul wrote to Timothy, his son in the faith, fellow worker in the gospel, and the person Paul left in Ephesus to pastor the local church there, including the church's **mission** and **message** all under the **Master**, Jesus Christ.

In 1 Timothy 3:1–13, Paul had been instructing Timothy on the qualifications for elders and deacons in the church. Then he said, "I am writing these things to you, hoping to come to you before long; but in case I am delayed, I write so that you will know how one ought to conduct himself in the household of God, which is the church of the living God, the pillar and support of the truth" (vv. 14–15).

It's interesting that Timothy was ministering in Ephesus, one of the great cities in Asia Minor. Ephesus was famous for its beautiful temple to the goddess Artemis, which was one of the Seven Wonders of the ancient world and one of the largest temples the Greeks ever built. The worship of Artemis was the center of life at Ephesus, as is obvious from the Ephesians' reaction when Paul came preaching the gospel and people started getting saved. The apostle stirred the city up so much that the people rushed into the arena and shouted, "Great is Artemis of the Ephesians!" for almost two hours (Acts 19:34).

But despite this intense opposition, the church was established in Ephesus and became a voice for the truth. Paul drew on this background in his instructions to Timothy. His purpose was to tell Timothy how people who belong to Christ and are part of His church ought to behave "in the household of God" (1 Tim. 3:15), which he identified as the church. Timothy knew how violently the pagans in Ephesus had conducted themselves when their goddess was threatened, but the conduct demanded of God's people is to be entirely different.

One thing that makes the church distinct from all other entities is our *Master*. Now don't misunderstand. God is the Master of the entire universe. "The earth is the LORD's, and all it contains, the world, and those who dwell in it" (Ps. 24:1). There is no one or nothing beyond God's control, even though most of the world does not acknowledge that fact. The Bible leaves no doubt as to who is in charge of God's church: Christ (see Col. 1:18). When Jesus returns to reign over this earth, every part of creation will bow to His Lordship, but until then Jesus is the recognized Master of the church.

The church is God's house, not ours. Our job as church leaders is not to make up the rules for the church, but to announce and teach God's rules outlined in His Word. His name is on the title deed to the church, because "He purchased [it] with His own blood" (Acts 20:28).

You would expect a living body with a distinctive Master to have a distinctive *mission*, and that's what we find with the church. Paul pointed to this mission when he told Timothy that the church is "the pillar and support of the truth" (1 Tim. 3:15).

Picturing the church as a pillar that helps to support a structure would have had vivid meaning to the people of Ephesus, because one notable feature of Artemis's fabulous temple was its lavishly decorated pillars. There were more than a hundred of these pillars supporting the temple, with all kinds of decorations on them in honor of various gods who supposedly joined the people in paying homage to the great Artemis.[1]

The problem was that the pillars in the temple of Artemis helped hold up a lie because Artemis was not the true God. There is only one source of truth in the universe, which Paul said elsewhere is found "in Jesus" (Eph. 4:21; John 14:6). And since Jesus has entrusted His Word of truth to the church (see John 17:17), the church is to be the guardian and disseminator

---

1. "The Temple of Artemis at Ephesus," Marmaris Info, accessed September 9, 2019, https://marmaris.info/about/the-temple-of-artemis-at-ephesus/.

of the truth. No other body of people on earth has been given this assignment to uphold truth.

Thus, the overarching mission of the church is to verbally and visibly testify to the truth of the one true God, based on His inherent Word, by making kingdom disciples. We as the people of God who have been united by Christ into one body are called to proclaim and live out the truth.

Truth is the only way to freedom even when that truth may be painful or inconvenient or lead to a struggle. Remember that Jesus said, "You will know the truth, and the truth will make you free" (John 8:32). The church's mission as a truth-teller cannot be compromised without leading people into error and eventual bondage to the lies of Satan (see John 8:44).

The church simply needs to convey God's truth in all of its clarity and power. Yes, we must also defend the truth from distortion and misrepresentation, but the best defense of truth is a good offense in which we are taking God's Word through the church to the ends of the earth. Jesus said in John 14:6, "I am truth," not "I know the truth" or "I have access to the truth." He is the personification and embodiment of all that is true, so when we proclaim Him to the world, we are giving people a sure standard against which to measure and judge all reality. Therefore, anything that does not line up to Jesus and the inherent Word of God is false.

The church is distinctive in its *message* because we are obligated to proclaim the truth even when no one else agrees or stands with us. Our society only wants convenient, comfortable truth that fits with people's preconceived ideas and biases. That means the church had better be doing a good job of upholding and imparting the truth. One way we do that is by learning and knowing the Word of God. You can't uphold or teach what you don't know. Paul exhorted Timothy, "Be diligent to present yourself approved to God as a workman who does not need to be ashamed, accurately handling the word of truth" (2 Tim. 2:15). We need to learn the truth before we can impart it to someone else. Church leaders bear the primary responsibility of preaching and teaching the truth to the congregants.

But along with learning goes the need to live the truth. In another of his pastoral epistles, Paul urged Titus, "Speak the things which are fitting for sound doctrine" (2:1). The following verses reveal why it was so important for Titus to teach sound doctrine. God was interested in the way the believers on Crete lived their lives. The goal of Titus's instruction was that Christians would "[show] all good faith so that they will adorn the doctrine of God our Savior in every respect" (v. 10).

To adorn means to decorate or dress something up in a way that makes it look nice and people are attracted to it. Local churches are to teach their members to "wear" God's truth by putting it on display in our daily lives. It's true that not everyone is looking for the truth, but many people will be attracted to believers whose lives correspond to truth.

The gospel is "the power of God for salvation to everyone who believes" (Rom. 1:16). God's Word will do its work in hearts if we simply proclaim it accurately and faithfully. And when our own lives—and the lives of our church members—line up with the truth, our message has even more impact because we become Exhibit A of what God can do.

CHAPTER EIGHT

THE EXPERIENCES

◆

I enjoy microwave popcorn, particularly while watching a good movie or football game. It is intriguing to watch the complete transformation of hard, coarse seeds into soft, delectable pieces of popcorn. This metamorphosis occurs because the microwave heats up the moisture resident in every corn seed until it turns to steam. Once it becomes steam, the pressure becomes so great that the shell can no longer contain the moisture and an explosion occurs. Environment is everything. When the microwave performs as it was intended to, the seeds of corn are transformed.

What a microwave is to popcorn, the local church is to the Christian. The local church is the context God has created to transform Christians into more faithful versions of what we were created and redeemed to be: followers of Christ.

Since all true believers possess the Holy Spirit and become Christ-followers at the moment of salvation, we have the internal moisture necessary for the ongoing transformation process to occur as we continually develop in our discipleship process. Therefore, if the transformation does not continue to produce spiritual growth and we become stagnant in our growth as Christ-followers, we can conclude that either the seeds are not in the proper environment, positioning themselves for ongoing transformation, or the microwave of the church is not functioning properly, producing spiritual heat so the pressure of the Holy Spirit gets hot enough to "pop" the believer, shaping the believer more and more into conformity with Christ (see Rom. 8:28–29). How else can we explain the existence of so many defeated, joyless, powerless, angry, bitter, empty, self-proclaimed Christians today?

I believe that the church's failure to produce disciples is largely to blame for the failure of so many churches. This failure has led to the rise of contemporary, secularized pop psychology with a Christian veneer, which charges exorbitant prices to do what the church should be providing as a natural outgrowth of its ministry. This thesis certainly does not exonerate individual believers from their personal responsibility to follow Christ down the road to discipleship. It does, however, recognize that in addition to personal responsibility, God has created a context for this process to occur. Just as microwaves that don't work are of little use to the seeds of corn, so churches that don't get sufficiently "hot" and don't perform properly won't see much success in producing disciples, authentic followers of Christ.

Few people would disagree that the greatest church in history was the first church, the church at Jerusalem in the early chapters of Acts. This church was on fire, possessed by the Holy Spirit, exploding on the scene on the Day of Pentecost. Acts 2 shows that this church made an impact not only on those within it but they also made a far-reaching impact that transformed those around them. It did this through four vital, Spirit-inspired experiences that are necessities for those who would follow Christ in discipleship. These four experiences are meant to operate simultaneously in our lives through the ministry of the local church as we grow and develop: ***outreach***, ***growing in the Word***, ***fellowship***, and ***worship***, which are laid out for us clearly in one key passage:

> They were continually devoting themselves to the apostles' teaching and to fellowship, to the breaking of bread and to prayer. Everyone kept feeling a sense of awe; and many wonders and signs were taking place through the apostles. And all those who had believed were together and had all things in common; and they began selling their property and possessions and were sharing them with all, as anyone might have need. Day by day continuing with

one mind in the temple, and breaking bread from house to house, they were taking their meals together with gladness and sincerity of heart, praising God and having favor with all the people. And the Lord was adding to their number day by day those who were being saved. (Acts 2:42–47)

OUTREACH

When the Holy Spirit came on Pentecost, the church became a catalyst for change. They offered themselves as a witness for Jesus Christ. As we have seen in an earlier chapter, *evangelism is one of the absolute necessities for being a disciple.* The most obvious event of the church's witness in Acts 2 was Peter's great Pentecost sermon. This is the same Peter who, just a few weeks earlier, was too scared to admit that he even knew Jesus. What changed Peter? Acts 2 tells us that the Holy Spirit had taken control of Peter. He was about to take off and soar in his spiritual life. He would experience things he had never experienced before because now he will be a faithful witness for Jesus Christ.

The Jewish authorities then ordered the apostles to stop preaching and teaching about Jesus, and they backed the order with threats (see Acts 4:18–21). So the apostles went straight to the church and reported exactly what the authorities had said. The church immediately went to prayer, reminding God of His power and the fact that all this was happening in His predetermined plan (see vv. 23–28).

Then notice the church's prayer request in verse 29: "And now, Lord, take note of their threats, and grant that Your bond-servants may speak Your word with all confidence." One of the things a strong church must do is disciple their members to be a strong witness for Jesus Christ. We must all seek God for the ability to "speak Your word with all confidence" when called upon to do so in our lives. Perhaps that is with coworkers, family members, friends or even in more organized outreach initiatives through the church, but we all must be ready to "give an account for the hope that is in" us (1 Peter 3:15).

One reason a lot of us don't share Christ is that we've lost our excitement about Christ. When He is exciting to you, you can't keep Him to yourself. When something dynamic occurs internally, you want to express it externally. The believers who received the Spirit on Pentecost became witnesses. The result of their witness and Peter's sermon on that unique day was the addition of 3,000 new believers to the body of Christ. Please notice that these 3,000 people did not come because of an evangelistic program. They came because God's people were overwhelmed by His Spirit. They were excited about Jesus.

The Spirit of God had so filled the people of God that they couldn't keep the faith to themselves. The result was an evangelistic masterpiece. This ought to be happening in our churches as we scatter out each week to witness for Christ wherever we go.

GROWING IN THE WORD

Along with their dynamic witness, these early believers were growing in their knowledge of God's Word. In Acts 2:42 we read, "they were continually devoting themselves to the apostles' teaching." How often were they doing this? This passage says it was "day by day" (v. 46), just as people were being saved day by day.

This is what might be called *the education of the church.* This is the process by which the Word of God gets off the page and into our lives. As a disciple of Jesus Christ, the Word of God is as necessary and desirable as food is for the body. It is Scripture that equips us to live the Christian life. Your mind is the key to becoming a disciple because you are what you think about (see Prov. 23:7). If you've got a messed-up mind, you're going to have a messed-up life. The body reflects the thought processes of the mind, and all of us have come into the Christian life with distorted minds, contaminated by a sinful world.

Our minds need to be renewed (see Rom. 12:2). Only then will our lives be transformed. I've discovered that when you try to change people's actions without changing their thinking, you only do a temporary, patchwork job. If you want to fix what you do, you must first fix how you think about what you do. A transformed mind comes through the study and application of the Word of God (see James 1:19–25).

The believers in Acts 2 devoted themselves to the apostles' teaching. If you and your parishioners are going to become disciples, you must have a dynamic experience with Scripture and empower your members to have the same. When it comes to our spiritual education, we have a divine Teacher—the Holy Spirit. Jesus said the Spirit would remind us of all that He taught (see John 14:26).

FELLOWSHIP

The third necessary experience in following Christ is also found in Acts 2:42. Along with devoting themselves to the apostles' teaching, the believers were devoted to fellowship. Biblical fellowship is not just coffee and donuts in Sunday school, or a meal in the fellowship hall. Fellowship is *the mutual sharing of our lives with other believers*. Church members will never grow to full maturity in Jesus Christ all by themselves. You cannot become a disciple of Jesus Christ independently of others which is why every believer should be expected to be an active member of a local church.

The local church is the "fireplace" where one "log," or member, touches another, and the fire is maintained. The church at Jerusalem not only shared their lives with one another, they shared their possessions as needs arose (vv. 44–45). That's part of fellowship too. If your church is getting dull spiritually, your members need to be in proximity to others who are on fire so their fire can ignite them. If your church is losing its spiritual fire, it's going to turn into ashes. As pastor, you need to make sure your members are vitally connected with other believers who desire to be on fire too. Fellowship is designed to keep the fire burning. There was no such thing as a non-churched Christian in the New Testament. They were in dynamic fellowship with each other. Remember, people can get good preaching and singing without coming to church. There are sermons and songs galore on radio, television, CDs, YouTube, and more—but what they can't get is biblical fellowship outside of the local church.

WORSHIP

The fourth experience in following Christ and developing kingdom disciples is worship. Again in Acts 2:42, the believers devoted themselves to "the breaking of bread and to prayer." They were going to the temple every day and praising God continually.

Worship is the furnace of the spiritual life. Worship *is the celebration of God for who He is and what He has done, and for what we are trusting Him to do.* The issue in worship is not necessarily what you get out of it, but what God gets out of it. Praising God, worshiping Him, and celebrating God for who He is and what He has done are the ways to get God's attention. God responds to our worship. In fact, God invites us to worship Him. He has taken the initiative.

You will be surprised at the way the Spirit of God will ignite your Christian life when worship becomes not an event, but an experience; not a program, but a way of life. That includes encouraging your congregants to both public and private worship because both are critical for a growing disciple of Christ.

Many of us want to quit when something goes wrong. But our spiritual ancestors didn't throw in the towel when their whole world went wrong. Why? Because many of them had what we don't have—a worshiping lifestyle. No matter what is wrong in your life, there is always a reason to worship and praise God. Now, praising God does not mean denying your problems. But what does Paul say? "Be anxious for nothing, but in everything by prayer and supplication with thanksgiving let your requests be made known to God" (Phil. 4:6). If you want God's power in your life, then worship must be part of your daily function: celebrating God, exalting Him for what He has done. As pastor or church leader, you must make sure that corporate worship is not just an addendum to your church's ministry but is at the center of it.

What happens when a church becomes full of witnessing, learning-the-Word, fellowshipping, worshiping kinds of kingdom disciples, and creates an environment for all four of these essentials to flourish? I guarantee, based on God's unchanging Word, that the church, its members, families, and communities will be progressing in spiritual discipleship. The early believers in the Acts 2 church we have been looking at had the four experiences going strong, and Scripture indicates that at least two things happened: They had spiritual power and they saw spiritual results. Acts 2:43 says, "Everyone kept feeling a sense of awe." They were amazed at the work of God that was going on in their midst. Everyone had a sense that God was at work in a mighty way.

What were the results? Selfishness began to fall by the way-side (Acts 2:44–45). They became concerned for one another. Many people were getting saved every day (v. 47). And much more. All of this resulted from the overflow of the spiritual growth that occurred as they experienced God through these four vital experiences both within and among them. As pastor, you bear the primary responsibility for equipping your leaders and members toward this vision of being a discipling church.

THE ORDINANCES IN THE CHURCH

The Bible recognizes two ordinances to be observed by the church: communion and baptism. These ordinances are not merely pictures to remind Christians of spiritual realities. They are also channels the Holy Spirit uses to confer the benefits of the new covenant to the followers of Jesus Christ.

The word *ordinances* refers to those rites that Jesus, the

Lord of the kingdom, commanded the church to observe to remind His people of their special relationship to Him, as well as the benefits that accrue because of this relationship.

They are also both signs of a new covenant. *Covenant* is the word that God uses to describe His relationship with His people. A covenant can be defined as *a spiritually binding relationship that God has with His people, bringing them the benefits of His kingdom.* A covenant is a divinely created relational bond through which God's kingdom operates. The old covenant was the Mosaic law that God gave to Israel. The new covenant is the covenant of grace that God has given to the church. This new covenant is based on God's new relationship to the church through the death and resurrection of Christ.

Under the old covenant, God related to His people by the principle of law. In the new covenant, God relates to His people by grace through the Holy Spirit. To help us understand and demonstrate His new covenant, God has given us these two biblical symbols of communion and baptism. These are pictures of Christ's death and resurrection.

Baptism

The ceremony of baptism is *the point at which your members go public with their testimony that they belong to Christ, and are committed to become a visible, verbal disciple of His.* Baptism is connected in Scripture to the old covenant of circumcision. Under the old covenant of the Mosaic law, all males had to be circumcised to become members of the covenant and share in its benefits; circumcision was the sign or symbol of the covenant.

But in the new covenant, the symbol is no longer physical in the sense of a cutting of the flesh, and it applies to all believers, not just males. We read in Colossians 2: "In (Christ) all the fullness of Deity dwells in bodily form, and in Him you have been made complete, and He is the head over all rule and authority; and in Him you were also circumcised with a circumcision made without hands, in the removal of the body of the flesh by the circumcision of Christ; having been buried with Him in baptism" (vv. 9–12).

God is saying that in the new covenant, entering into the covenantal relationship is a spiritual transaction that is demonstrated, or symbolized, through baptism. Thus baptism is the new "circumcision" whereby the believer publicly identifies with Christ. It not only says that we have accepted Jesus as Savior but are committed to coming under His kingdom authority as Lord. Such public identification is critical for us to experience the blessings and benefits of the new covenant that are conferred by the Holy Spirit.

And in baptism, we see a picture of our burial and resurrection with Christ (Romans 6:3–4). They are symbols for the saved to understand and experience our unique spiritual connection to, and the benefits of, this new covenant God has with us.

Because baptism is a spiritual covenant, Jesus told His disciples in the Upper Room, "I will ask the Father, and He will give you another Helper, that He may be with you forever; that is the Spirit of truth, whom the world cannot receive, because it does not see Him or know Him, but you know Him because He abides with you and will be in you" (John 14:16–17).

Communion

The second biblical ordinance of the church is communion, which is *the ongoing renewal of the new covenant that was inaugurated at baptism*, just as Passover was the renewal of the old covenant. The Bible makes this connection in 1 Corinthians 5:7 where Paul wrote, "Christ our Passover also has been sacrificed." Passover, of course, was the meal the Jews ate in Egypt the night the death angel came and killed the firstborn sons in all the homes of Egypt (see Ex. 12).

God's people avoided this plague by killing a lamb and putting its blood on the doorposts of their homes. The blood of the lamb was a symbol of the blood that Christ would shed on the cross to save us from the eternal spiritual death of eternal separation from God—and so Paul could refer to Christ as our Passover lamb.

Jesus consciously connected Passover with communion when He told the disciples at the beginning of the Last Supper, "I have earnestly desired to eat this Passover with you before I suffer" (Luke 22:15). Jesus knew that the time had come for Him to become the final sacrifice for sins.

On the night before His crucifixion, Jesus instituted the ordinance of communion in the upper room with His disciples. As He blessed and passed the cup, the Lord said, "This cup which is poured out for you is the new covenant in My blood" (Luke 22:20). The cup represents Christ's blood shed on the cross for our salvation. The bread of communion pictures and intimately connects us with Christ's body that was broken for us. The apostle Paul quoted Jesus' words as he explained the significance of communion in 1 Corinthians 11: "This is My body, which is for you; do this in remembrance of Me" (v. 24).

Communion is also referred to as the Lord's Supper, or the Lord's Table, a reference to 1 Corinthians 10:21, "You cannot drink the cup of the Lord and the cup of demons; you cannot partake of the table of the Lord and the table of demons." Did you realize there are two tables in the world? There is the table of the Lord and the table of demons. You can sit at one table or the other, but not at both. To sit at the table of the Lord is to sit in God's presence and remind yourself of His covenant and become a partaker of the benefits of being part of it as you submit to His kingdom authority in your life and share in His special spiritual power and presence (1 Cor. 10:16–17). You cannot do that and still fellowship at the table of the world. When you take communion, you identify yourself publicly with Christ and actually participate in a spiritual reality.

The celebration of communion is also a declaration of Christ's victory over sin, death, and the grave. In John 6:51 Jesus said, "I am the living bread that came down out of heaven; if anyone eats of this bread, he will live forever; and the bread also which I will give for the life of the world is My flesh."

Communion is also about reaching into heaven to draw down the spiritual and physical benefits and blessings attached to Christ's covenantal death and resurrection (Isa. 53:4–5, 1 Cor. 10:16–17). It is also an opportunity to let the enemy know he no longer holds authority over you. In chapter 11 of 1 Corinthians we read, "For as often as you eat this bread and drink the cup, you *proclaim the Lord's death* until He comes" (1 Cor. 11:26). The question that comes out of that verse is: Proclaim the Lord's death to whom? And for what reason?

To proclaim something is similar to preaching it. Paul writes that when you take communion, you are preaching. Pastor, you aren't the only one who is to be preaching on Sunday. *Your members* are to be preaching a sermon when they take communion. And the audience they are preaching their sermon to is found in Colossians, chapter 2. We read,

> When you were dead in your transgressions and the uncircumcision of your flesh, He made you alive together with Him, having forgiven us all our transgressions, having canceled out the certificate of debt consisting of decrees against us, which was hostile to

us; and He has taken it out of the way, having nailed
it to the cross. When He had disarmed the rulers and
authorities, He made a public display of them, having
triumphed over them through Him. (Col. 2:13–15)

Communion is your members' time to preach their sermons to the evil principalities and remind them that these
evil principalities have been defeated. It is your church's turn
to serve notice on Hell, based on the cup and the bread, that
Hell has already lost.

As believers, communion is one of the most, if not the most,
strategic things we can do. As a pastor, your role is to ensure
that your members have the opportunity to take communion
regularly and that they understand what they are doing. One of
the worst things you can do as a pastor is to make ritual what is
supposed to be sacred. Don't ever allow the experiential ordinances of baptism and communion, something so completely
profound, turn into something so completely ordinary.

Just as Adam and Eve lost victory and authority when they
disobeyed and ate the fruit wrongly, through communion we
eat in remembrance of Jesus and what He accomplished on
the cross and proclaim the regaining of the victory and the
authority that was originally lost.

APPENDIX

———————— ◆ ————————

MINISTRY OVERVIEW

The Urban Alternative (TUA) equips, empowers, and unites Christians to impact *individuals, families, churches,* and *communities* through a thoroughly kingdom agenda worldview. In teaching truth, we seek to transform lives.

The core cause of the problems we face in our personal lives, homes, churches, and societies is a spiritual one; therefore, the only way to address it is spiritually. We've tried a political, social, economic, and even a religious agenda.

It's time for a **kingdom agenda**.

The kingdom agenda can be defined as the visible manifestation of the comprehensive rule of God over every area of life.

The unifying central theme throughout the Bible is the glory of God and the advancement of His kingdom. The conjoining thread from Genesis to Revelation—from beginning to end—is focused on one thing: God's glory through advancing God's kingdom.

When you do not have that theme, the Bible becomes disconnected stories that are great for inspiration but seem to be unrelated in purpose and direction. The Bible exists to share God's movement in history toward the establishment and expansion of His kingdom highlighting the connectivity throughout which is the kingdom. Understanding that increases the relevancy of this several-thousand-year-old manuscript to your day-to-day living, because the kingdom is not only then, it is now.

The absence of the kingdom's influence in our personal and family lives, churches, and communities has led to a deterioration in our world of immense proportions:

- People live segmented, compartmentalized lives because they lack God's kingdom worldview.
- Families disintegrate because they exist for their own satisfaction rather than for the kingdom.

- Churches are limited in the scope of their impact because they fail to comprehend that the goal of the church is not the church itself, but the kingdom.
- Communities have nowhere to turn to find real solutions for real people who have real problems because the church has become divided, in-grown and unable to transform the cultural landscape in any relevant way.

The kingdom agenda offers us a way to see and live life with a solid hope by optimizing the solutions of heaven. When God, and His rule, is no longer the final and authoritative standard under which all else falls, order and hope leaves with Him. But the reverse of that is true as well: As long as you have God, you have hope. If God is still in the picture, and as long as His agenda is still on the table, it's not over.

Even if relationships collapse, God will sustain you. Even if finances dwindle, God will keep you. Even if dreams die, God will revive you. As long as God, and His rule, is still the overarching rule in your life, family, church, and community, there is always hope.

Our world needs the King's agenda. Our churches need the King's agenda. Our families need the King's agenda.

In many major cities, there is a loop that drivers can take when they want to get somewhere on the other side of the city, but don't necessarily want to head straight through downtown. This loop will take you close enough to the city so that you can see its towering buildings and skyline, but not close enough to actually experience it.

This is precisely what we, as a culture, have done with God. We have put Him on the "loop" of our personal, family, church, and community lives. He's close enough to be at hand should we need Him in an emergency, but far enough away that He can't be the center of who we are.

We want God on the "loop," not the King of the Bible who comes downtown into the very heart of our ways. Leaving God on the "loop" brings about dire consequences as we have seen in our own lives and with others. But when we make God, and His rule, the centerpiece of all we think, do or say, it is then that we will experience Him in the way He longs to be experienced by us.

He wants us to be kingdom people with kingdom minds set on fulfilling His kingdom's purposes. He wants us to pray, as Jesus did, "Not my will, but Thy will be done." Because His is the kingdom, the power, and the glory.

There is only one God, and we are not Him. As King and Creator, God calls the shots. It is only when we align ourselves underneath His comprehensive hand that we will access His full power and authority in all spheres of life: personal, familial, church, and community.

As we learn how to govern ourselves under God, we then transform the institutions of family, church, and society from a biblically based kingdom worldview.

Under Him, we touch heaven and change earth.

To achieve our goal, we use a variety of strategies, approaches, and resources for reaching and equipping as many people as possible.

BROADCAST MEDIA

Millions of individuals experience *The Alternative with Dr. Tony Evans* through the daily radio broadcast playing on nearly **1,400 radio outlets** and in over **130 countries**. The broadcast can also be seen on several television networks, and is viewable online at TonyEvans.org. You can also listen or view the daily broadcast by downloading the Tony Evans app for free in the App store. Over 18,000,000 message downloads/streams occur each year.

LEADERSHIP TRAINING

The Tony Evans Training Center (TETC) facilitates educational programming that embodies the ministry philosophy of Dr. Tony Evans as expressed through the kingdom agenda. The training courses focus on leadership development and discipleship in the following five tracks:

- Bible and Theology
- Personal Growth
- Family and Relationships
- Church Health and Leadership Development
- Society and Community Impact Strategies

The TETC program includes courses for both local and online students. Furthermore, TETC programming includes course work for non-student attendees. Pastors, Christian leaders and Christian laity, both local and at a distance, can seek out The Kingdom Agenda Certificate for personal, spiritual and professional development. For more information, visit: tonyevanstraining.org

The Kingdom Agenda Pastors (KAP) provides a *viable network* for *like-minded pastors* who embrace the Kingdom Agenda philosophy. Pastors have the opportunity to go deeper with Dr. Tony Evans as they are given greater biblical knowledge, practical applications, and resources to impact individuals, families, churches, and communities. KAP welcomes *senior and associate pastors* of all churches. KAP also offers an annual Summit held each year in Dallas with intensive seminars, workshops and resources.

Pastors' Wives Ministry, founded by Dr. Lois Evans, provides *counsel, encouragement,* and *spiritual resources* for pastors' wives as they serve with their husbands in the ministry. A primary focus of the ministry is the KAP Summit that offers senior pastors' wives a safe place to *reflect, renew,* and *relax* along with training in personal development, spiritual growth, and care for their emotional and physical well-being.

COMMUNITY & CULTURAL INFLUENCE

National Church Adopt-A-School Initiative (NCAASI) prepares churches across the country to impact communities by using *public schools as the primary vehicle for effecting positive social change* in urban youth and families. Leaders of churches, school districts, faith-based organizations, and other nonprofit organizations are equipped with the knowledge and tools to *forge partnerships* and build *strong social service delivery systems.* This training is based on the comprehensive church-based community impact strategy conducted by Oak Cliff Bible Fellowship. It addresses such areas as economic development, education, housing, health revitalization, family renewal, and racial reconciliation. We assist churches in tailoring the model to meet specific needs of their communities while simultaneously addressing the spiritual and moral frame of reference. Training events are held annually in the Dallas area at Oak Cliff Bible Fellowship.

Athlete's Impact (AI) exists as an outreach both into and through the sports arena. Coaches are the most influential factor in young people's lives, even ahead of their parents. With the growing rise of fatherlessness in our culture, more young people are looking to their coaches for guidance, character development, practical needs, and hope. After coaches on the influencer scale fall athletes. Athletes (whether professional or amateur) influence younger athletes and kids within their spheres of impact. Knowing this, we have made it our aim to equip and train coaches and athletes on how to live out and utilize their God-given roles for the benefit of the kingdom. We aim to do this through our iCoach App as well as resources such as The Playbook: A Life Strategy Guide for Athletes.

Tony Evans Films ushers in positive life change through compelling video-shorts, animation and feature-length films. We seek to build kingdom disciples through the power of story. We use a variety of platforms for viewer consumption and have over 35,000,000 digital views. We also merge video-shorts and film with relevant Bible Study materials to bring people to the saving knowledge of Jesus Christ and to strengthen the body of Christ worldwide. Tony Evans Films released our first feature-length film, *Kingdom Men Rising*, in April, 2019 in over 800 theaters nationwide, in partnership with Lifeway Films.

RESOURCE DEVELOPMENT

We are fostering lifelong learning partnerships with the people we serve by providing a variety of published materials. Dr. Evans has published more than 100 unique titles based on over 40 years of preaching whether that is in booklet, book, or Bible study format. He also holds the honor of writing and publishing the first full-Bible commentary and Study Bible by an African American, released in 2019.

For more information, and a complimentary copy
of Dr. Evans's devotional newsletter, call (800) 800-3222
or write TUA at P.O. Box 4000, Dallas TX 75208,
or visit us online at www.TonyEvans.org

ACKNOWLEDGMENTS

———————— ♦ ————————

I am extremely grateful to the Moody Publishers family for their partnership with me in the development of this series of books for pastors and ministry leaders. Special thanks go to Greg Thornton who has been with me on this publishing journey with Moody Publishers from the start. I also want to thank Heather Hair for her collaboration on this manuscript. I want to acknowledge the Tony Evans Training Center, under the leadership of John Fortner, for the use of some course material which appears in this book. No book comes to life without editorial assistance, and so my thanks also includes Michelle Sincock and Duane Sherman.

Building Kingdom Disciples

At The Urban Alternative, eternity is our priority—for the individual, the family, the church and the nation. The nearly 50-year teaching ministry of Tony Evans has allowed us to reach a world in need with:

The Alternative – Our flagship radio program brings hope and comfort to an audience of millions on over 1,400 radio outlets across the country.

tonyevans.org – Our library of teaching resources provides solid Bible teaching through the inspirational books and sermons of Tony Evans.

Tony Evans Training Center – Experience the adventure of God's Word with our online classroom, providing at-your-own-pace courses for your PC or mobile device.

Tony Evans app – Packed with audio and video clips, devotionals, Scripture readings and dozens of other tools, the mobile app provides inspiration on-the-go.

Go deeper in
your biblical studies
with Dr. Tony Evans. Learn
how to share the gospel with
CONFIDENCE.

MORE FROM
THE KINGDOM PASTOR'S LIBRARY

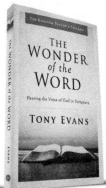

978-0-8024-1831-9

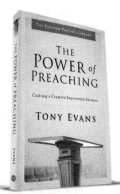

978-0-8024-1830-2

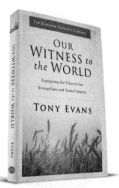

978-0-8024-1833-3

The Kingdom Pastor's Library is a series that brings you a concise,
complete pastoral philosophy and training from Tony Evans.

Faithful. Powerful. Practical. Become a Kingdom Pastor today.

also available as eBooks and audiobooks

MOODY
Publishers®

From the Word to Life®

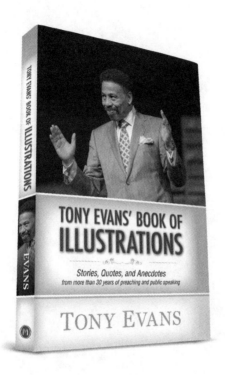